Make a Monster

Make a Monster

15 easy-to-make fleecie
toys you'll love to sew

Fiona Goble

NEW
HOLLAND

First published in 2010 by New Holland Publishers (UK) Ltd

London · Cape Town · Sydney · Auckland

Garfield House, 86–88 Edgware Road

London W2 2EA, United Kingdom

www.newhollandpublishers.com

80 McKenzie Street, Cape Town 8001, South Africa

Unit 1, 66 Gibbes Street, Chatswood, NSW 2067, Australia

218 Lake Road, Northcote, Auckland, New Zealand

ISBN 978 1 84773 596 6

Publisher: Clare Sayer

Photography: Mark Winwood

Production: Marion Storz

Design: Zoe Mellors and Sarah Gardner

Editorial Direction: Rosemary Wilkinson

10 9 8 7 6 5 4 3 2 1

Reproduction by Pica Digital Pte Ltd, Singapore

Printed and bound by Craft Print International Ltd, Singapore

Safety note
Some of the projects in this book are unsuitable for children under 3 years of age due to small parts. Always keep small or sharp objects (such as needles or buttons) away from small children.

Contents

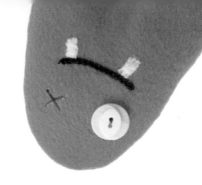

Introduction

If you want to stitch yourself a troupe of quirky new friends, then this is the book for you. The cute creatures in this collection are all made from easy-to-sew fleece fabric which is widely available in a great range of colours. And if you want to help the planet and save money at the same time, why not recycle old fleece clothes into brand new fleecie friends?

For starters, there are Wilf, Prudence and Melvin – three lovable little misfits. They're small enough to fit in your pocket and travel with you everywhere. Then there's flowery-eyed Dilly who looks as if butter wouldn't melt in her mouth and lolloping Dotty who thinks she's a heart throb. There are loads more besides, all waiting to be sewn into your ideal companions. You can even use the patterns in this book to develop your own unique monsters.

I've marked all the projects according to how easy they are. The ones marked with one star are the easiest and the ones marked with three stars the most challenging. But even if you're new to sewing, the clear photographs, instructions and useful tips mean that you'll almost certainly be able to make all of the projects in this book with just a little practice.

These monsters would make great gifts – not just for children but also for older children and even adults with a sense of humour. But it's also nice to sew something for yourself once in a while.

So sit back and take a look through the book and choose your favourites. Then decide exactly what fabric and trimmings you're going to use to create your very first monster. I hope you have fun!

Fiona Goble

Tools and Materials

TOOLS

Before you start making these fleecie monsters you will need to check out your sewing box and general supplies for some basic equipment and tools. You are bound to have some of the items you need already but there may be some things you will need to borrow or buy.

Photocopier or computer with scanner and printer, plus a supply of thick paper or thin card and some sticky tape.

The templates on pages 98–127 are shown actual size. The easiest and most accurate way to transfer the templates is to photocopy them onto thin card or thick paper. Alternatively, you can scan them into your computer then print them out. In some cases the templates have been split over two pages; simply join at the dotted lines and tape together.

Sewing machine and sewing machine needles

You can easily sew the fleecie monsters and any clothes and accessories by hand but a sewing machine will make it much quicker. A machine that does zig zag stitch is useful for some of the monsters but one that simply does running stitch will also be fine. Your machine should be fitted with a needle suitable for medium weight fabrics. A standard European size 70 or 80 (US 11 or 12) needle is ideal.

It's a good idea to have a few available as machine needles can bend or become blunt quite easily and you may need to replace them fairly often.

Needles for hand sewing

You will need two types of hand sewing needles to make the monsters – a standard sewing needle and an embroidery needle.

You will need a standard sewing needle (a 'sharp') if you are hand sewing your monsters and accessories. Even if you are sewing by machine you will need this type of needle for closing the openings used for stuffing, attaching some of the arms and legs and sewing some of the monsters' features.

You will need an embroidery or crewel needle for stitching some of the monsters' facial features. This type of needle is a sharp, medium length needle that has an eye large enough for you to thread embroidery thread.

Iron

You will need an iron when making some of the monsters and their clothes, to press open seams and to fix bonding web and appliqués.

Water-soluble pen or quilter's pencil

You will need a water-soluble pen or quilter's pencil to draw round the templates and to mark some of the monsters' features before you sew them. They work like ordinary felt pens or pencils but the marks are easily removed by spraying or dabbing with water. The pens usually come in bright blue and are the best option for marking light and medium coloured fabrics. For darker fabrics, choose one of the pencils which come in a range of light colours, including white and yellow. These pens and pencils

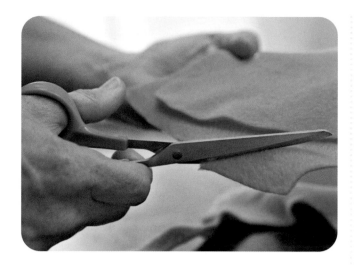

are widely available in craft and haberdashery shops, and through mail order and internet companies that supply accessories for patchwork and quilting.

Ordinary pencil

You will need a pencil for tracing some of the appliqué shapes onto the backing paper of your bonding web (see page 10). A pencil is sometimes also useful for pushing the toy filling into the monsters' limbs.

Scissors

Ordinary scissors are fine for cutting your template card or paper but you need a pair of good quality sewing scissors for cutting fabric. You will also need some sharp embroidery scissors for cutting out small items such as the felt eyes featured in some of the projects. Make sure that you keep your sewing and embroidery scissors strictly for cutting fabric and threads as using them on card or paper will quickly blunt them.

Dressmaking pins

You will need a small number of dressmaking pins to pin your work together before basting or sewing. It is a good idea to use pins with coloured glass ends

as they are easier to see and less likely to get left in your work by mistake.

Tape measure

This will be useful for checking the size of your fabric pieces before beginning your project.

Piece of fine cotton

To protect your work, you will need a piece of fine cotton, such as a handkerchief, when ironing the appliqués in position.

Safety pin

You will need a small safety pin to thread the elastic through the casing of some of the monsters' clothes.

Stitch ripper and tweezers

These tools will come in handy if you make a mistake and need to undo your work. A stitch ripper has a point on the end and a sharp blade and will enable you to undo stitching without the risk of cutting or pulling the fabric. They are widely available in craft and haberdashery shops. Tweezers are useful for picking out any cut stitches that remain in your work.

MATERIALS

All the materials you need to make the monsters are available in dress fabric shops and haberdashery stores or from mail order and internet companies. The main fabric used for the creatures themselves is polyester fleece – sometimes called 'polar fleece'. This is the fabric used to make items such as fleece tops, hats and scarves. You will also need polyester toy filling to stuff your monsters and small quantities of felt and embroidery threads for their features. Depending on which creature you are making, you may also need other types of fabric and a selection of trimmings, including buttons. The exact requirements for each monster are given on the individual project pages.

Fleece fabric

The monsters are all made from standard fleece fabric, sometimes called 'polar fleece'. Fleece is available in a variety of thicknesses and finishes. Medium weight fleece with a slight pile is ideal for making fleecie creatures as thin fabrics can be too stretchy and thick fabrics too difficult to work with.

Good quality fleece fabric usually has a pile which makes it smoother when you stroke it in one direction than any other. It is important when making the creatures that the direction of the pile runs down the length of the creature.

Fleece fabric in a good range of colours is available in many dress fabric shops, and there are some attractive patterned designs as well. But if there isn't a good fabric shop near you, don't worry. There are plenty of mail order and internet companies offering this type of fabric at competitive prices (see Suppliers on page 128), and it is often available through individual sellers and stores on Ebay.

If you want an even greater choice of colours and textures – and want to save money at the same time – you could look at fleece clothing in budget and second hand shops. You could even give your own old clothes a second lease of life by transforming them into fleecie monsters!

Polyester filling

This 100 per cent polyester filling is manufactured specially for stuffing soft toys, cushions and other handmade items. It is widely available in craft and haberdashery shops. Always check that the filling you are buying is marked safe and washable and that it conforms to safety standards.

Patterned cottons

For some of the monsters you will need small amounts of printed fabrics in 100 per cent cotton or cotton mixes (a blend of polyester and cotton). You don't need to use exactly the same fabric shown in the project. But the fabric you use will determine the finished look and character of your monster, so spend a bit of time selecting a fabric that you really like and that you think will work well.

Felt

Felt is used for some of the monsters' features. There are two main types of craft felt, both of them widely

available and sold in squares measuring about 23 x 23 cm (9 x 9 in) in craft, haberdashery and fabric shops. The first type is made from 100 per cent polyester and the second type from a mixture of viscose and wool. I would recommend that you try to find the felt made from viscose and wool because it is slightly thinner and easier to cut into small shapes. Some craft shops also sell ready-cut felt circles and shapes which you may find useful for the creatures' eyes in some of the projects.

Embroidery thread

Some of the monsters' features are embroidered with 100 per cent cotton stranded embroidery thread. This is made up of six strands that can be easily separated. Most of the projects use either six or three strands.

Sewing thread

Whether you are sewing with a machine or by hand, you will need standard sewing threads to match your fabrics. Threads made from 100 per cent polyester, often called 'all purpose' are widely available and come in a good range of colours. While it is not essential to go for the very best quality threads, it is important to avoid very poor quality, cheap threads as they can break easily and are prone to puckering.

Elastic

A few of the projects require narrow elastic or elastic cord that is threaded through the waistbands of clothes. This is widely available and comes in black or white. As it will not usually show, it doesn't really matter which colour you use.

Bonding web

For some of the creatures you will need a small amount of fusible bonding web to fasten the appliqués. Bonding web is a thin web of dry glue that is fixed on a paper backing. The shape for the appliqué is traced onto the paper backing with a normal pencil. The bonding web is then ironed onto the reverse side of the fabric and cut out. The backing can then be peeled off and the appliqué pressed in place with an iron. There are several brands of bonding web on sale and it is widely available in craft and haberdashery shops.

Seam sealant

Seam sealant is a special type of clear liquid that comes in a small bottle with a pointed nozzle with a narrow opening. It is used in some of the projects to prevent trimmings from fraying. Although the sealant is fine to use on most trimmings, it is a good idea to test it on a scrap of the trimming first. Seam sealant is widely available in craft and haberdashery shops.

Trimmings and buttons

For some of the projects you will need buttons, ribbons and other trimmings. You should be able to find a good selection of these in your local craft or haberdashery shop or at internet companies that specialise in fabrics and trimmings or card making. Second hand stores are also a great source of these items – especially buttons. The trimmings you select are crucial to your project and choosing the right ones will help make sure that your fleecie monsters look great. So take your time when deciding which ones to use. You will find it really helpful if you build up your own collection as this will enable you to try out various styles before deciding which is your favourite.

SAFETY

It is very important that you do not give any of the monsters with added extras, such as buttons, to children under three years old as these can be a choking hazard. All of the creatures can be easily adapted to suit younger children. For example, you can use eyes made from coloured circles of felt instead of buttons.

Techniques

PREPARING YOUR TEMPLATES

All the templates you need for making the monsters in this book are on pages 98–127. All templates are shown actual size. The easiest way to prepare your template is to use a photocopier or to scan it into a computer using a flat bed scanner. Simply photocopy the templates you need onto thick paper or thin card or scan them into your computer and print them out onto thick paper or thin card. In some cases the templates have been split over two pages; simply join at the dotted lines and tape together.

TRANSFERRING YOUR TEMPLATE TO YOUR FABRIC

You can transfer your template to your fabric by holding the template firmly in position on the reverse side of your fabric and drawing round it using a water-soluble pen or quilter's pencil. You can use the same pen or pencil to mark the positions of the dots which act as guidelines for sewing and making your monsters. Simply poke the pen nib or pencil tip through the template or make a hole in the template first using a large needle.

BASIC SEWING SKILLS

If you are sewing your monsters by machine, you will need to use a medium length straight stitch to sew your monsters together and to stitch their clothes. The instructions for some of the monsters also recommend that you use zig zag stitch if your machine has this option, though this is not essential. If you are using zig zag stitch, it is a good idea to test it out first on a scrap of material so you can check that you are pleased with the size and spacing of the stitching.

If you are sewing by hand, use a standard 'sharps' sewing needle and a small running stitch. Work a small back stitch every few stitches for extra strength.

To secure your work at the beginning and end, work a few stitches on top of each other if you are sewing by hand. If you are using a sewing machine, most machines have a reverse direction so you can sew a short length of reverse stitching before you begin and after you complete your sewing to secure the stitches in place.

Basting

Because fleece is not a slippery fabric, most of the monsters can be completed by simply pinning the pieces of work together before sewing. For some steps in some of the projects, however, it is easier if you baste your fabric first. Basting stitches are temporary stitches that are pulled out after your work is finished. They are large running stitches and, so long as they are holding your work in position securely, they do not have to be particularly even or tidy. It is sensible to baste in a contrasting thread colour so that you can easily tell which threads to pull out.

Sewing your monster using corresponding pieces

This book uses a slightly different technique for sewing pieces together than many other books. For example, instead of cutting two pieces of a main body shape, you are asked to cut just one piece and then to cut a corresponding shape – a second piece of fabric that roughly matches the original piece. You place your original piece face down on this corresponding piece before seaming the pieces together. Then you trim your fabric to match your shape before turning your work the right way out.

Sewing your toys in this way is both quicker and easier. And even if you aren't an experienced sewer, you can achieve great results because you won't find holes in your seams or uneven work, even if your fabric has slipped or stretched slightly.

Stuffing

Always use a small amount of toy filling at a time when you are stuffing your monsters. Also, try not to push each bit in too hard or your creature will look lumpy. The monsters should look fully stuffed but have a nice squashy feel. You can push the stuffing into the creatures using the blunt end of a pencil or something similar – but make sure that you don't use anything too sharp or push too hard or you might break the stitching.

Slip stitch and closing openings

Once your monster has been turned the right way out and stuffed, you will need to close the opening that you have used for stuffing. The neatest way is to slip stitch the two edges together. Fold in the raw edges on both sides of the opening, in line with the seam line. From the inside, bring your needle out

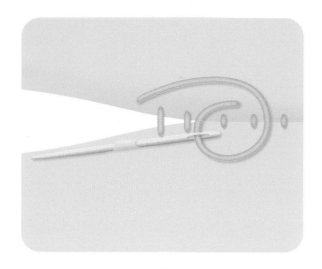

hand. It is also used for joining some of the creatures' limbs to their main bodies. Use small stitches along the fabric edge or across two pieces of fabric to join them together. Once the thread is pulled fairly tightly, the stitches should be virtually invisible on fleece. In the case of felt features, use the point of a fine needle to tease the fabric around the stitches to make them barely noticeable.

Hemming stitch

If you are using a sewing machine, you can use a small zig zag stitch or a normal straight stitch to

through one side of the fold at the beginning of the opening. Take the needle in through the fold directly opposite and out through the same fold, about 3 mm (⅛ in) further along. Work a few stitches at a time before pulling your thread taut. You will also need to work similar slip stitches to turn up some of the creatures' feet.

Oversewing

This stitch is used to fasten some of the felt and fleece features such as the monsters' eyes, and to sew on some of the appliqués if you are sewing by

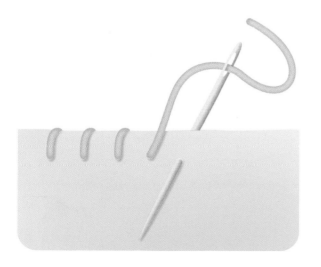

hem the monsters' clothes. If you are sewing by hand, it is best to use a hemming stitch. This is a bit like slip stitch. Begin by fastening your thread to the folded hem allowance. Pick up a thread or two of the garment using the point of your needle. Then take your needle back into the folded edge of the hem and out again about 5 mm (¼ in) further along, ready for the next stitch.

SPECIAL EMBROIDERY STITCHES

For some of the monsters you will need to use special embroidery stitches. Instructions for these stitches are given below.

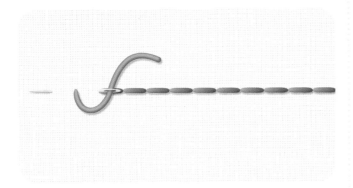

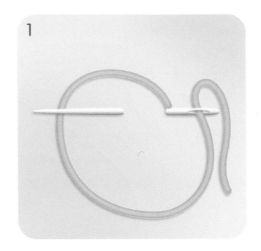

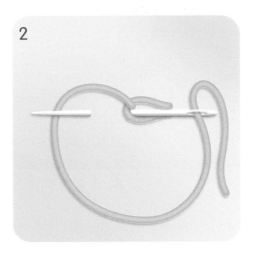

Back stitch (see above)

This is used to work some of the monsters' mouths. To work a row of back stitch, bring your thread out at your starting point and start by working a single running stitch. Insert your needle back into the end point of the first stitch then out again, a little further on from the end of the last stitch.

Chain stitch (see right)

This is used to work some of the monsters' mouths and some of their teeth. First, bring your needle out at the point where you want the chain to start. Insert the needle back into the same hole and out at the point you want the stitch to end – about 2 or 3 mm ($\frac{1}{8}$ in) further on – making sure the thread is under the needle point (step 1). Now pull the thread through. You are now ready to start the second stitch (step 2). At the end of the row, make a small stitch over the last loop to hold it in position (step 3). If you are just working single chain stitches, simply make the small loop over the single stitch to hold it in position.

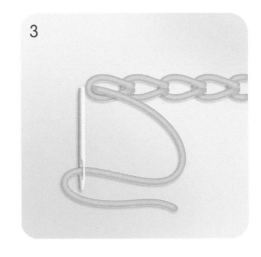

Blanket stitch (see right)

You will use this stitch round the edge of some of the appliquéd pieces on the creatures if you are sewing by hand, as an alternative to machine zig zag stitching. To begin, take your needle out at your starting point. Then insert your needle back through your fabric, a stitch width to the side. Now bring the needle round the back of the edge, directly above this point (step 1). Make sure your thread is under the needle point and pull up gently to make the first stitch (step 2). Work round the edge of the piece in the same way, taking care to make your stitches the same height and width (step 3).

1

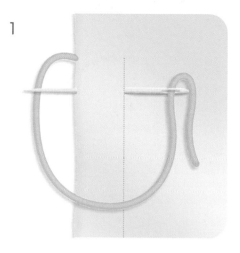

2

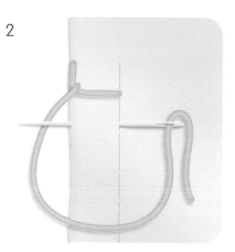

3

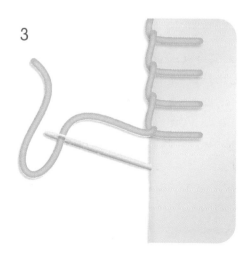

A NOTE ON MEASUREMENT

All the measurements in this book are given in metric units (millimetres or centimetres) with the measurement in inches and fractions of an inch given in brackets afterwards. It is difficult to convert small measurements exactly so figures have been rounded up or down, usually to the nearest $\frac{1}{4}$ in. Because it is impossible to make the conversions exact, it is important that you follow one system only rather than mix the two.

Part sleepy rabbit and part creature from another planet, Toby has the sweetest of natures. Because he's so soft and cuddly, he would make an ideal gift for babies and young children. As a bonus, he's also one of the easiest fleecie monsters to make.

∗∗ Quite easy

MATERIALS

- a piece of bright yellow fleece measuring 36 x 40 cm (14 x 16 in). If the fabric has an obvious pile this should run down its longer length.
- a scrap of printed cotton or cotton mix fabric for the face
- a small piece of bonding web
- 30 g (1 oz) of polyester toy stuffing
- matching threads for your fabrics
- black sewing thread for machine stitching the facial features (or black embroidery thread if you want to sew the features by hand)

TOOLS

- access to a photocopier or computer with scanner and printer
- scissors
- sewing needles
- dressmaking pins
- water-soluble pen or quilter's pencil
- ordinary pencil
- sewing machine (optional)
- iron
- a piece of fine cotton such as a handkerchief to protect the appliqué when fixing with the iron

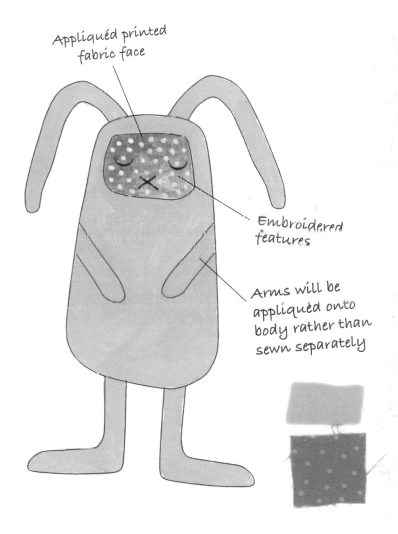

Appliquéd printed fabric face

Embroidered features

Arms will be appliquéd onto body rather than sewn separately

Toby is approximately 25 cm (10 in) tall

TO MAKE THE MONSTER

1 Photocopy or scan the templates on pages 98–99 and cut them out (you do not need to cut out the face template). Place the yellow fleece right side down on a flat surface. Position your templates and draw round them with the water-soluble pen or quilter's pencil. You will need to cut out one body shape, two leg shapes and two ear shapes. Make sure that any pile on the fabric runs down the length of the pieces in the direction of the arrows

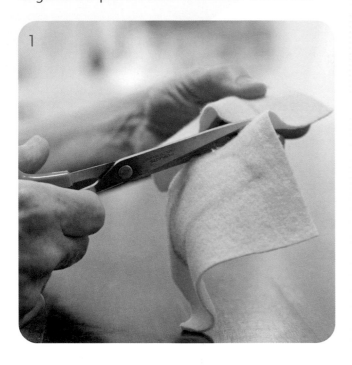

shown on the templates and remember to mark the position of the dots. You will also need to cut shapes that roughly match these pieces (for more information, see page 12), bearing in mind the direction of the pile. Now cut out two arm pieces, making sure that the pile runs down the length of the pieces, in the direction of the arrow. You will need to cut one arm shape using the template the right way up and the other using the template face down.

2 To make the appliquéd face, trace round the face template onto the backing paper of a piece of bonding web using an ordinary pencil. Next, with the iron on a warm setting, iron the bonding web onto the reverse of your piece of cotton or cotton mix fabric and cut the shape out carefully. Peel off the backing paper and position the face on the body shape, as shown on the template. Place a piece of fine cotton over the template and iron to fix. Sew round the face using a small zig zag stitch if your machine has this option. Alternatively, use an ordinary machine running stitch. If sewing by hand, use a small blanket stitch (see page 15) worked with your thread double.

3 Position the arms on the body piece, as shown on the template. Pin or baste in position. Sew round the edges of the arms using a small zig zag stitch if your machine has this option. Alternatively, use a small blanket stitch worked with your thread double.

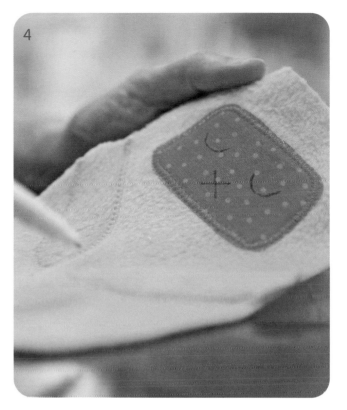

4 Draw the facial features onto the face with the water-soluble pen or quilter's pencil, using the template as a guide. Machine stitch the features using a fairly long running stitch. You will need to work about six rows of stitching along and then back on the same line to make sure the features stand out sufficiently strongly. Alternatively, embroider the features by hand using back stitch (see page 14) and three strands of black embroidery thread.

6 Sew the two legs in the same way that you sewed the ears. Turn them the right way out and stuff.

5 Place one of the ear shapes onto its corresponding piece of fleece, making sure that the right sides are together and any obvious pile on the corresponding fabric is going in the same direction as the main piece. Sew round the ear shape 5 mm (¹/₄ in) from the edge, leaving the flat end open for turning. Complete the second ear in the same way. Trim away the excess fabric on the corresponding pieces of fleece so that they match the original ear shapes. Turn the ears the right way out but do not stuff.

7 Pin the ears to the main body piece between the dots at the top of the head, so that the flat end of the ears lines up with the top of the head and the ears point right down the body. Baste in position. Now place the body piece face down on its corresponding piece of fleece, making sure that the

pieces are right sides together and any obvious pile on the corresponding fabric is going in the same direction as the main piece. Sew round the body piece 5 mm (¼ in) from the edge, leaving openings between the dots for inserting the legs and turning and stuffing. Trim away the excess fabric. Turn the body the right way out and stuff. Close the opening used for turning and stuffing using slip stitch (see page 12).

8 Insert about 5 mm (¼ in) of the top of one of the legs into one of the openings at the bottom of the body. The leg seams should run down the front and back of the legs, rather than each side. Secure by oversewing across the front and back of the leg top (see page 13). Insert and secure the other leg in the same way.

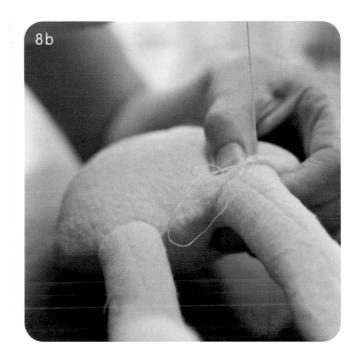

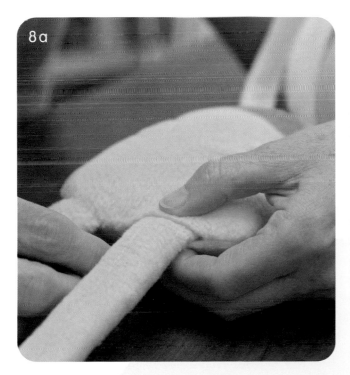

9 To make the feet, turn up 8 cm (3¼ in) at the end of each leg and hold in place so that the foot is at a right angle to the leg. Now, using the thread double for strength and starting at one of the side seams, work a few large, loose slip stitches (see page 12) across the curve at the front of the ankle. Pull up the thread fairly tightly and secure.

✳ COOL IDEA

Make sleepy Toby a cuddly blanket by hemming round the edges of a 30-cm (12-in) square of contrasting fleece.

Dilly

Cute Dilly with her flower petal eyes and retro print skirt has something of the flower fairy about her. It's easy to imagine her sitting among the flower pots and relaxing in the garden. But I'm sure she'd feel just at home in any little girl's bedroom.

✳✳ Quite easy

MATERIALS

- a piece of mid-pink fleece measuring 32 x 34 cm (12½ x 13½ in). If the fabric has an obvious pile this should run down its shorter length.
- a scrap of pale pink fleece for the face
- a scrap of turquoise felt for the eyes
- two yellow buttons approximately 18 mm (¾ in) diameter for the eyes
- a 24 x 11 cm (9½ x 4½ in) piece of patterned cotton or cotton mix fabric for the skirt. If the pattern has an obvious direction this should run up or down the shorter length of the fabric.
- a 15-cm (6-in) length of narrow elastic or elastic cord for the skirt waistband
- red embroidery thread for the mouth
- 30 g (1 oz) polyester toy stuffing
- matching threads for your fabrics (except turquoise felt)

TOOLS

- access to a photocopier or computer with scanner and printer
- scissors
- sewing needles
- dressmaking pins
- small safety pin for threading the elastic
- water-soluble pen or quilter's pencil
- sewing machine (optional)
- iron

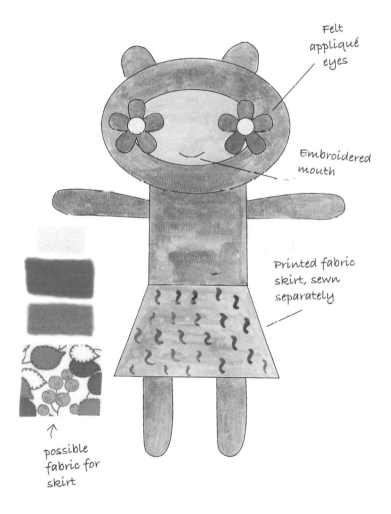

Felt appliqué eyes

Embroidered mouth

Printed fabric skirt, sewn separately

↑ possible fabric for skirt

Dilly is approximately 27 cm (10½ in) tall

TO MAKE THE MONSTER

1 Photocopy or scan the templates for making Dilly on pages 100–101 and cut them out. Place the mid-pink fleece right side down on a flat surface. Position your templates and draw round them with the water-soluble pen or quilter's pencil. You will need to cut out one body shape and two arm shapes. Make sure that any pile on the fabric runs down the length of the pieces in the direction of the arrows shown on the templates and remember to mark the position of the dots. You will also need to cut shapes that roughly match these pieces (for more information, see page 12), bearing in mind the direction of the pile. From the pale pink fleece, cut out one face panel.

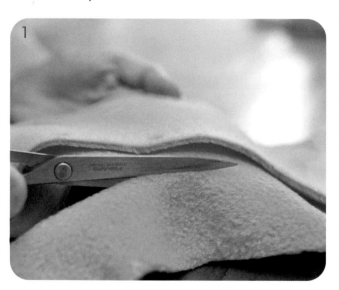

2 Place the face panel on the head as shown on the template, making sure that any obvious pile goes downwards, and pin or baste in position. Sew round the face using a small zig zag stitch if your machine has this option. Alternatively, use an ordinary machine stitch or oversew by hand (see page 13). If sewing by machine, it's a good idea to start your stitching in the middle of one side of the face so any join will be hidden by the felt flower eye.

3 Using the water-soluble pen or quilter's pencil, draw the mouth onto the face panel using the template as a guide. Embroider the mouth in back stitch (see page 14) using six strands of red embroidery thread.

3

5

4 Place one of the arm pieces onto its corresponding piece of fleece, making sure that the right sides are together and any obvious pile on the corresponding fabric is going in the same direction as the main piece. Sew round the arm shape 5 mm (¼ in) from the edge, leaving the flat end open for turning and stuffing. Trim away the excess fabric on the corresponding piece of fleece so that it matches the original arm shape. Complete the second arm in the same way. Turn the arms the right way out and stuff.

5 Now place the body piece face down on a corresponding piece of fleece, making sure that the pieces are right sides together and any obvious pile on the corresponding fabric is going in the same direction as the main piece. Sew round the body piece 5 mm (¼ in) from the edge, leaving openings between the dots for inserting the arms and for turning and stuffing. Trim away the excess fabric. Turn the body the right way out and stuff. Close the opening used for turning and stuffing using slip stitch (see page 12).

4

6 Insert about 5 mm (¼ in) of the top of one of the arms into the opening at the side of the body. Secure by oversewing across the front and back of the arm top (see page 13). Position and secure the other arm in the same way.

7 Using the template, cut out two flower shapes from turquoise felt using small embroidery scissors. Using the photo of the finished monster as a guide, position the flower eyes in place and secure using the yellow buttons and contrasting sewing thread.

FOR THE SKIRT

1 Fold the rectangle of fabric in half widthways so that the pattern is on the inside, and stitch the back seam leaving a 5-mm (¼-in) seam allowance. Press the seam open. For the hem, turn under 1 cm (⅜ in) at the bottom edge and press in place. Turn up another 1 cm (⅜ in) and press again. Stitch close to the folded edge using a machine running stitch or hand hemming stitch (see page 13).

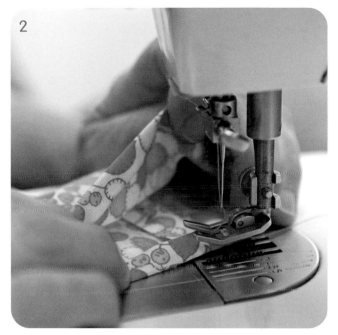

2 For the waistband casing, prepare the fabric as for the hem but, when sewing, leave a 1-cm (⅜-in) opening at the back seam for threading the elastic. Using the small safety pin, thread the elastic through the casing. Adjust the elastic so that the skirt will fit securely round the monster's waist and trim if necessary. Overlap the ends of the elastic and stitch together securely – or knot the ends together tightly.

*COOL IDEA

To give Dilly a really whacky look, use different buttons for her eyes and decorate her skirt with rows of lace and ric rac tape.

Quincy

Quincy is one unique fleecie creature! He has all the fluffy appeal of a favourite teddy bear – but there's a definite hint of octopus in him as well. Although he looks as if he'd be hard to put together, Quincy is made from just two main pattern pieces – so please give him a go.

** Quite easy

MATERIALS

- a piece of orange fleece measuring 35 x 35 cm (14 x 14 in)
- a scrap of lime fleece for the face
- scraps of black and white felt for the eyes
- a 5-cm (2-in) length of 15-mm (¾ in) wide yellow ric rac braid
- 20 g (¾ oz) polyester toy stuffing
- matching threads for your fabrics including the felt, plus red thread for the mouth
- seam sealant for preventing ric rac from fraying (optional)

TOOLS

- access to a photocopier or computer with scanner and printer
- scissors
- sewing needles
- dressmaking pins
- water-soluble pen or quilter's pencil
- sewing machine (optional)

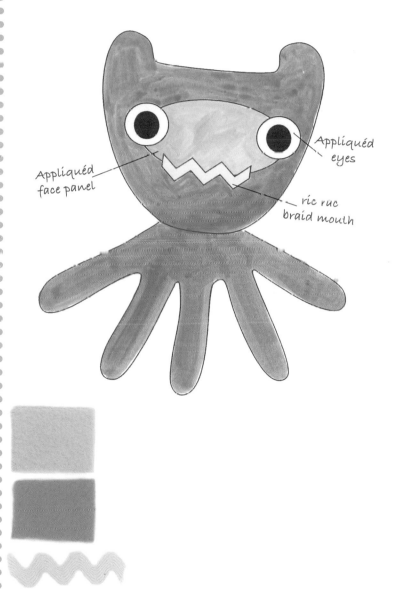

Appliquéd face panel

Appliquéd eyes

ric rac braid mouth

Quincy is approximately 15 cm (6 in) tall

TO MAKE THE MONSTER

1 Photocopy or scan the templates for making Quincy on pages 102–103 and cut them out. Place the orange fleece right side down on a flat surface. Position your templates and draw round them with the water-soluble pen or quilter's pencil. You will need to cut out one head shape and one leg shape, remembering to mark the position of the dots. For the head shape, make sure that any pile on the fabric runs down the length of the piece in the direction of the arrows shown on the template. You will also need to cut shapes that roughly match these pieces (for more information, see page 12), bearing in mind the direction of the pile. From the lime fleece, cut out one face panel.

2 Place the face panel on the head as shown on the template, making sure that any obvious pile goes downwards, and pin or baste in position. Sew round the face using a small zig zag stitch if your machine has this option. Alternatively, use an ordinary machine stitch or oversew by hand (see page 13). If you are sewing by machine, it's a good idea to start your stitching in the middle of one side of the face so any join will be hidden by the felt eye.

3 Treat the ends of the ric rac braid with seam sealant and leave till completely dry. Meanwhile, use the templates to cut out two outer eyes in white felt and two inner eyes in black felt. Using the template as a guide, oversew the eyes in place using tiny stitches (see page 13). When you have finished, gently tease round the stitches with the tip of your needle so that the stitches become almost invisible.

4 Using the photograph as a guide, now pin or baste the ric rac braid mouth in position. Machine stitch along the middle of the ric rac braid using red thread. Work two rows, one on top of the other, to make sure the stitching stands out. If sewing by hand, back stitch (see page 14) along the braid using your thread double.

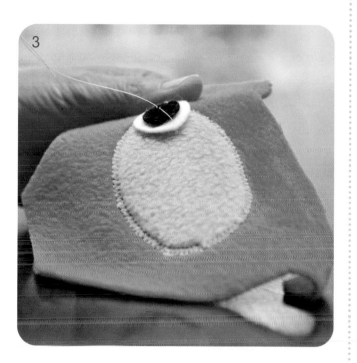

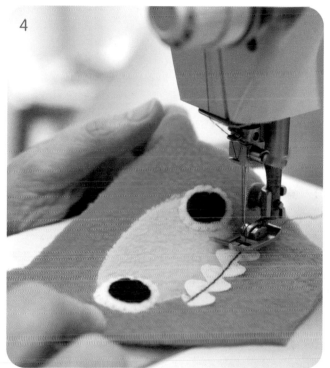

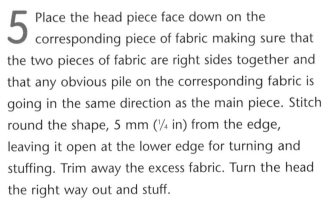

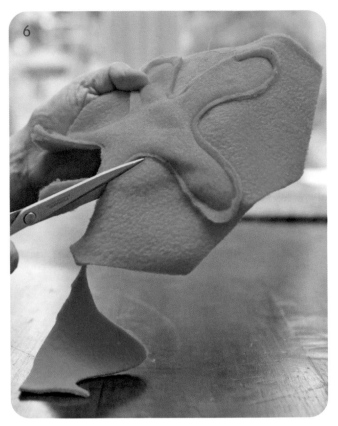

5 Place the head piece face down on the corresponding piece of fabric making sure that the two pieces of fabric are right sides together and that any obvious pile on the corresponding fabric is going in the same direction as the main piece. Stitch round the shape, 5 mm (¼ in) from the edge, leaving it open at the lower edge for turning and stuffing. Trim away the excess fabric. Turn the head the right way out and stuff.

6 Place the leg piece face down on the corresponding piece of fabric making sure that the two pieces of fabric are right sides together. Stitch round the shape, 5 mm (¼ in) from the edge, leaving an opening between the dots for turning and stuffing. Trim away the excess fabric. Turn the leg piece the right way out and stuff. Close the opening used for turning and stuffing using slip stitch (see page 12).

7 Place the head piece onto the centre of the leg piece and slip stitch in position (see page 12), slightly opening out the neck edge as you go so that the base of the neck forms a circle shape on the top of the leg piece.

8 Working from the underneath, fold each leg up slightly. Using your thread double for strength, sew a few large slip stitches (see page 12) across the fold of each leg to secure in position.

7a

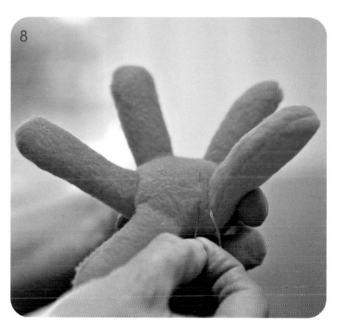

8

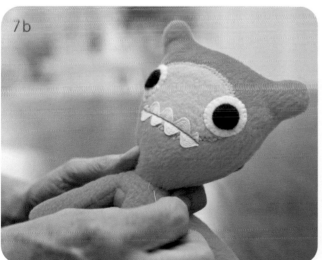

7b

✳COOL IDEA

To give Quincy a skittish look, try sewing some of his legs folded down and some folded upwards.

Ned and Son

Thoughtful and loyal are the words that best sum up Ned, this little blue creature from some strange planet or other. He displays his character in the heart on his chest and is just dying to be made and become your faithful companion.

✳ Really easy

MATERIALS

- a piece of bright blue fleece measuring approximately 42 x 32 cm (16½ x 12½ in). If the fabric has an obvious pile this should run down its shorter length.
- a scrap of lime green fleece for the heart
- scraps of bright pink and white felt
- two medium and two small odd buttons for the eyes
- red embroidery thread for the mouth
- a small piece of bonding web
- 30 g (1 oz) polyester toy stuffing
- matching threads for your fabrics including the felt

TOOLS

- access to a photocopier or computer with scanner and printer
- scissors
- sewing needles
- dressmaking pins
- water-soluble pen or quilter's pencil
- ordinary pencil
- sewing machine (optional)
- iron
- a piece of fine cotton such as a handkerchief to protect the appliqué when fixing with the iron

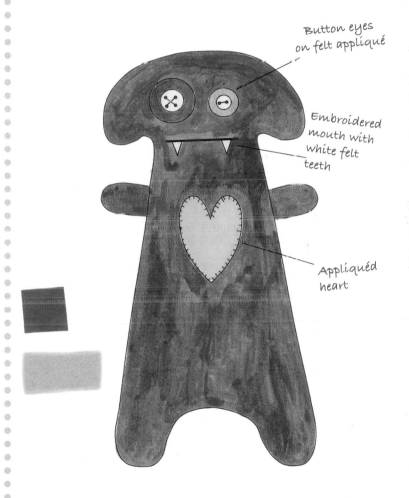

Button eyes on felt appliqué

Embroidered mouth with white felt teeth

Appliquéd heart

Ned is approximately 26 cm (10¼ in) tall and his son is approximately 18 cm (7 in) tall

TO MAKE THE MONSTER

1 Photocopy or scan the templates for making Ned on pages 104–105 and cut them out (you do not need to cut out the heart template). Place the blue fleece right side down on a flat surface. Position your template and draw round it with the water-soluble pen or quilter's pencil. You will need to cut out just one body shape at this stage. Make sure that any pile on the fabric runs down the length of the piece in the direction of the arrow shown on the template and remember to mark the position of the dots. You will also need to cut a shape that roughly matches the body piece (for more information, see page 12), bearing in mind the direction of the pile.

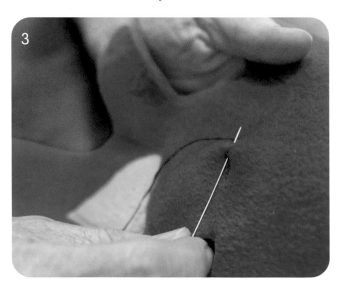

2 To make the heart appliqué, trace round the heart template onto the backing paper of a piece of bonding web using an ordinary pencil. Next, with the iron on a warm setting, iron the bonding web onto the reverse of your piece of lime fleece and cut the shape out carefully. Peel off the backing paper and position the appliqué on the body, as shown on the template. Place a piece of

fine cotton over the template and iron to fix. You might find it easier to iron on the reverse of the body piece to do this. Sew round the appliqué using a small zig zag stitch if your machine has this option. Alternatively, use an ordinary machine running stitch or oversew by hand (see page 13).

3 Using the template as a guide, embroider the mouth in chain stitch (see page 14) using three strands of red embroidery thread. Cut two small

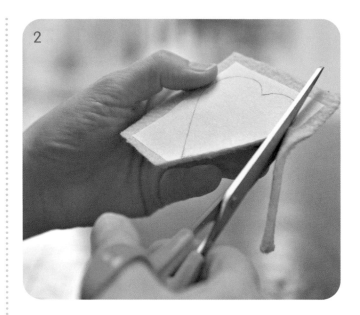

triangles from the scrap of white felt for the teeth and oversew these in position using tiny stitches (see page 13). Using the template, cut out one eye patch shape from the pink felt. Position as shown on the template and oversew in place using tiny stitches. When you have finished, gently tease round the stitches on the teeth and eye patch with the tip of a needle so that your stitches become almost invisible.

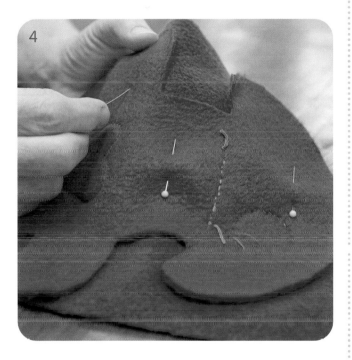

4 Now place the body piece face down on the corresponding piece of fleece, making sure that the pieces are right sides together and any obvious pile on the corresponding fabric is going in the same direction as the main piece. Sew round the body piece 5 mm (¼ in) from the edge, leaving an opening between the dots for turning and stuffing. Trim away the excess fabric. Turn the body the right way out and stuff. Close the opening used for turning and stuffing using slip stitch (see page 12).

5 Using the photograph as a guide, place the two small buttons on the two larger buttons and sew in position using contrasting thread.

✱COOL IDEA

To make Ned's son, reduce the pattern by about one-third on a photocopier or computer. Make in exactly the same way as for Ned only omit the eye patch, work the teeth in single chain stitch, and try to keep your seam allowance to approximately 3 mm (⅛ in).

Mungo

Mungo is cheerful and cheeky with a great eye for fashion. With his huge eyes, Mungo will keep a watch over you wherever you are.

✳✳✳ Some sewing experience helpful

MATERIALS

- a piece of turquoise fleece measuring 46 x 29 cm (18 x 11½ in). If the fabric has an obvious pile this should run down its shorter length.
- scraps of red and black fleece for the eyes
- a 14 x 28 cm (5½ x 11 in) piece of printed cotton or cotton mix fabric for the shorts
- a 15-cm (6-in) length of narrow elastic or elastic cord for the waistband of the shorts
- 30 g (1 oz) polyester toy stuffing
- thin black wool or embroidery thread for the nose and mouth
- matching threads for your fabrics

TOOLS

- access to a photocopier or computer with scanner and printer
- scissors
- sewing needles
- dressmaking pins
- small safety pin for threading the elastic
- water-soluble pen or quilter's pencil
- sewing machine (optional)
- iron

Appliquéd eyes

Embroidered mouth and nose

Printed shorts

OR

Mungo is approximately 26 cm (10¼) tall

TO MAKE THE MONSTER

1 Photocopy or scan the templates for making Mungo on pages 106–107 and cut them out. Place the turquoise fleece right side down on a flat surface. Position your templates and draw round them with the water-soluble pen or quilter's pencil. You will need to cut out one body shape and two arm shapes. Make sure that any pile on the fabric runs down the length of the pieces in the direction of the arrows shown on the templates and remember to mark the position of the dots. You will also need to cut shapes that roughly match these pieces (for more information, see page 12), bearing in mind the direction of the pile.

2 Using the eye templates, cut out two outer eye shapes from the red fleece and two inner eye shapes from the black fleece. For both eye pieces, you will need to cut out one shape using the template the right way up and one shape using the template face down.

3 Position the eye pieces as shown on the template and pin then baste in place. (Basting is a good idea here as it is important the eyes are sewn on in identical positions on both sides of the face, or your creature's eyes will look uneven.) Sew the eyes along the inside edges only, using a small zig zag stitch if your machine has one. Alternatively use a machine running stitch or oversew by hand (see page 13).

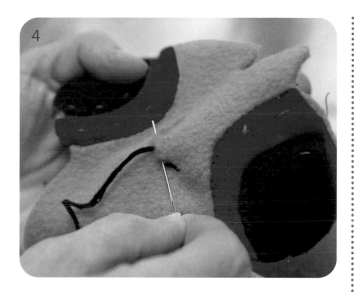

4 Using the template as a guide, draw the nose and mouth using a water-soluble pen or quilter's pencil. Now sew the nose and mouth using the thin black wool or six strands of black embroidery thread using a fairly large back stitch (see page 14).

5 Fold the body piece in half lengthways so that the fleecie side of the fabric is on the inside.

Sew the body dart – from the centre of the lower end of the face into the neck then from the neck outwards to the tummy – using a small running stitch or medium length machine stitch.

6 Place one of the arm pieces onto its corresponding piece of fleece, making sure that the right sides are together and any obvious pile on the corresponding fabric is going in the same direction as the main piece. Sew round the arm

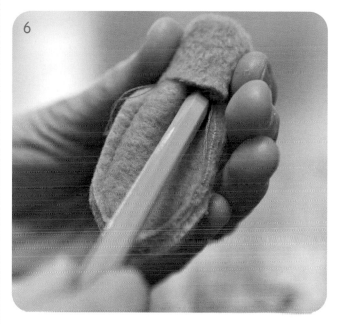

shape 5 mm (¼ in) from the edge, leaving the flat end open for turning and stuffing. Trim away the excess fabric on the corresponding piece of fleece so that it matches the original arm shape. Complete the second arm in the same way. Turn the arms the right way out and stuff.

7 Now place the body piece face down on its corresponding piece of fleece, making sure that the pieces are right sides together and any obvious pile on the corresponding fabric is going in the same direction as the main piece. Sew round the body

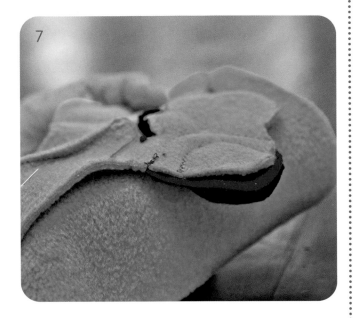

piece 5 mm (¼ in) from the edge, leaving openings between the dots for inserting the arms and for turning and stuffing. Trim away the excess fabric. Turn the body the right way out and stuff. Close the opening used for turning and stuffing using slip stitch (see page 12).

8 Insert about 5 mm (¼ in) of the top of one of the arms into the opening at the side of the body. Secure by oversewing across the front and back of the arm top (see page 13). Position and secure the other arm in the same way.

FOR THE SHORTS

1 Photocopy the shorts template on page 107 and cut it out. Use the template to cut out two shapes from patterned cotton or cotton mix fabric, making sure any directional pattern will lie the right way on the finished shorts. Lay the two pieces of fabric right

sides together and sew the crotch seams, allowing a 5-mm (¼-in) seam allowance. Press the seams open with the iron.

2 Keeping the right sides of the fabric facing, match the front and back crotch seams and stitch the inside leg seams, again allowing a 5-mm (¼-in) seam allowance. Press the seams open.

3 Turn under 1 cm (⅜ in) at the end of each leg and press in place. Turn up another 1 cm (⅜ in) and press again. Stitch close to the folded edge using a machine running stitch or hand hemming stitch (see page 13).

4 To make the waistband, turn under 1 cm (⅜ in) at the top raw edge and press in place. Turn down another 1 cm (⅜ in) and press again. Stitch as close as possible to the folded edge, leaving a 1 cm (⅜ in) opening at the back of the shorts for threading the elastic. Using the small safety pin, thread the elastic cord through the waistband casing. Adjust the elastic so that the shorts will fit securely round the creature's waist and trim if necessary. Overlap the ends of the elastic and stitch together securely – or knot the ends together tightly.

*COOL IDEA

For a girly fleecie monster in this style, make this creature in pink or mauve and sew her a skirt as given for Dilly on page 27.

Cuddly Martha with her flowery tummy patch loves the countryside. She probably likes nothing better than hopping about the fields and wildflowers on her big feet. But something tells me she'd feel just as much at home on a nice flowery pink quilt or soft cushion.

Martha

*** Some sewing experience helpful

MATERIALS

- a piece of bright pink fleece measuring 28 x 40 cm (11 x 16 in). If the fabric has an obvious pile this should run down its longer length.
- a piece of pale pink fleece measuring 21 x 17 cm (8¼ x 6¾ in). If the fabric has an obvious pile this should run down its longer length.
- scraps of black and white felt for the eyes
- a small piece of medium weight cotton or cotton/linen mix floral print fabric for the tummy patch and ears
- a small piece of bonding web
- a small black button for the nose
- dark grey embroidery thread
- 35 g (1¼ oz) polyester toy stuffing
- matching threads for your fabrics and felt

TOOLS

- access to a photocopier or computer with scanner and printer
- scissors
- ordinary pencil
- sewing needles
- dressmaking pins
- water-soluble pen or quilter's pencil
- sewing machine (optional)
- iron
- a piece of fine cotton such as a handkerchief to protect the appliqué when fixing with the iron

Printed fabric ears

Appliqué and embroidery eyes

Embroidered mouth and button nose

Arms will be separate from body and seamed in at front

Printed fabric patch

'vintage' fabric Could use this or perhaps a paisley

Martha is approximately 25 cm (10 in) tall

TO MAKE THE MONSTER

1 Photocopy or scan the templates for making Martha on pages 108–109 and cut them out (you do not need to cut out the tummy patch template). Place the bright pink fleece right side down on a flat surface. Position your templates and draw round them with the water-soluble pen or quilter's pencil. You will need to cut out two body

pieces, two leg and two arm pieces. Make sure that any pile on the fabric runs down the length of the pieces in the direction of the arrow shown on the templates and remember to mark the position of the dots. You will also need to cut shapes that roughly match the arm and leg pieces (for more information, see page 12), bearing in mind the direction of the pile. From the pale pink fleece, cut out two head pieces. Cut out four ear pieces from your floral fabric.

2 To make the tummy appliqué, trace round the tummy patch template onto the backing paper of a piece of bonding web using an ordinary pencil. Next, with the iron on a warm setting, iron the bonding web onto the reverse of your piece of fabric and cut the shape out carefully. Peel off the backing paper and position the patch on the body, as shown on the template. Place a piece of fine cotton over the template and iron to fix. You might find it easier to iron on the reverse of the body piece to do this. Sew round the appliqué using a small zig zag stitch if your machine has this option. Alternatively, use an ordinary machine running stitch. If sewing by hand, use a small blanket stitch (see page 15) worked with your thread double.

3 Use the templates to draw and cut out two outer eyes from white felt and two inner eyes from black felt with the small embroidery scissors. Using the template as a guide, oversew the eyes in place using tiny stitches (see page 13). Using the template as a guide again, embroider the mouth in chain stitch (see page 14) using three strands of dark grey embroidery thread. You will find it easier to sew if you draw an outline using your water-soluble pen or quilter's pencil before you begin. Make a row of five separate, large running stitches for the eyelashes, again using three strands of dark grey embroidery thread. Sew on the button nose.

4 Place one of the arm pieces onto its corresponding piece of fleece, making sure that the right sides are together and any obvious pile on the corresponding fabric is going in the same direction as the main piece. Sew round the arm shape 5 mm (¼ in) from the edge, leaving the flat end open for turning. Trim away the excess fabric on the corresponding piece of fleece so that it matches

the original arm shape. Complete the second arm and both legs in the same way. Turn the arms and legs the right way out and stuff the legs but not the arms.

5 Place two of the ear pieces right sides together and sew round the curved edge leaving a 5-mm (¼-in) seam allowance. Make small snips into the seam allowance, taking care not to cut the stitching (this will help give the finished ear a smooth shape). Turn the ear the right way out and press. Complete the second ear in the same way.

6 Seam the head piece with the facial features to the body piece with the tummy patch, catching in the arms where indicated on the template, and leaving a 5-mm (¼-in) seam allowance. Seam the back head and body pieces together in the same way, leaving a gap between the dots for stuffing.

7 For the ears, fold the two lower corners towards the middle so that, for the left-hand ear, the left corner overlaps the right and, for the right-hand ear, the right corner overlaps the left.

8 Baste the ears onto the head piece in the position indicated on the template, lining up the flat raw edge of the ears with the raw edge at the top of the head so that the ears point down the head. Place the two body pieces right sides together, checking that the side seams line up, and stitch round the complete creature in matching threads 5 mm (¼ in) from the edge, leaving openings between the dots for inserting the legs. Turn the right way out through the gap at the back. Stuff your creature then slip stitch the opening closed (see page 12).

9 Insert about 5 mm (¼ in) of the top of one of the legs into the opening at the bottom of the body. Secure by oversewing across the front and back of the leg top (see page 13). Position and secure the other leg in the same way.

10 To make the feet, turn up 6 cm (2½ in) at the end of each leg and hold in place so that the foot is at a right angle to the leg. Now, using the thread double for strength and starting at one of the side seams, work a few large, loose slip stitches (see page 12) across the curve at the front of the ankle. Pull up the thread fairly tightly and secure.

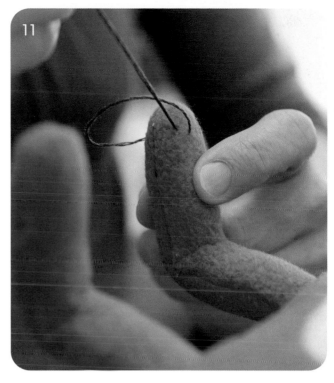

11 For the claws, use three strands of dark grey embroidery thread. Secure the thread invisibly in the side seam and take the needle out through the top of the foot ready to sew the first claw. Now take the thread over the end of the foot, through the back and out through the top again, ready to work the next claw. Work two more claws the same way and secure the thread in the side seam.

❋COOL IDEA

For a cat-like version of Martha, try sewing two simple triangular ears instead of the bunny-like ears shown here.

Dinah's ancestors were clearly dinosaurs. But with her soft pink spikes and colourful eye, Dinah is a whole lot less scary than her prehistoric forebears. However she still likes to scream and shout a bit.

Dinah and Daughter

MATERIALS

- a piece of bright green fleece measuring 30 x 40 cm (12 x 16 in). If the fabric has an obvious pile this should run down its shorter length.
- a piece of mid-pink fleece measuring 17 x 6 cm (6¾ x 2½ in)
- a scrap of yellow felt for the eye
- a 15-mm (¾-in) button for the eye
- 30 g (1 oz) polyester toy stuffing
- matching threads for your fabrics except the yellow felt

TOOLS

- access to a photocopier or computer with scanner and printer
- scissors
- sewing needles
- dressmaking pins
- water-soluble pen or quilter's pencil
- sewing machine (optional)

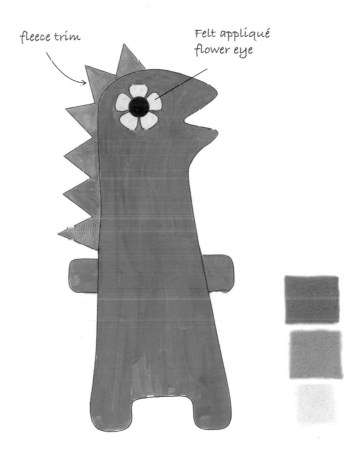

fleece trim

Felt appliqué flower eye

Dinah is approximately 29 cm (11½ in) tall and her daughter is approximately 21 cm (8¼ in) tall

TO MAKE THE MONSTER

Alternatively, use a straight machine or hand running stitch. Trim very close to the stitching using embroidery scissors, taking care not to cut the stitching itself.

1 Photocopy or scan the templates for making Dinah on pages 110–111 and cut them out. Place the green fleece right side down on a flat surface. Position your template and draw round it with the water-soluble pen or quilter's pencil. You will need to cut out just one body shape at this stage. Make sure that any pile on the fabric runs down the length of the piece in the direction of the arrow shown on the template and remember to mark the position of the dots. You will also need to cut a shape that roughly matches the body piece (for more information, see page 12), bearing in mind the direction of the pile.

2 Draw round the spikes template on the reverse side of the pink fleece using the water-soluble pen or quilter's pencil but do not cut out just yet. Sew just inside the cutting line of the spikes using a small zig zag stitch if you are using a sewing machine and your machine has this facility.

3 Lay the spikes down on the right side of the body shape, between the dots on the template, so that the spikes face inwards and the flat edge lines up with the flat edge of the body. If your fleece has an obvious front and back and you want a monster facing right (like Dinah), make sure that you

lay the spikes right sides up when you pin them to the body. For a monster facing left (like Dinah's daughter), lay the spikes right side down. Baste the spikes in position.

4 Now place the body piece face down on the corresponding piece of fleece, making sure that the pieces are right sides together and any obvious pile on the corresponding fabric is going in the same direction as the main piece. Sew round the body piece 5 mm (¼ in) from the edge, leaving an opening between the dots for turning and stuffing. Trim away the excess fabric. Turn the body the right way out and stuff. Close the opening used for turning and stuffing using slip stitch (see page 12).

5 For Dinah's eye, use the template to cut out a flower shape from the yellow felt using small embroidery scissors. Using the template as a guide, position the flower eye in place and secure using the button.

Playful Leo does his best to snarl and adopt a menacing stance and he'd like people to think he was really scary. But, as everyone knows, he's just a big softie – and actually, he's not even all that big!

Leo

MATERIALS

- a piece of bright red fleece measuring 34 x 45 cm (13½ x 17¾ in). If the fabric has an obvious pile this should run down its longer length.
- a scrap of beige fleece for the face
- a scrap of pale pink felt for the mouth
- two medium odd buttons for the eyes
- lime green embroidery thread for the claws
- 20 g (¾ oz) polyester toy stuffing
- matching threads for your fabrics including the felt
- black sewing thread for machine stitching the mouth (or black embroidery thread if you want to sew the features by hand)

TOOLS

- access to a photocopier or computer with scanner and printer
- scissors
- sewing needles
- dressmaking pins
- water-soluble pen or quilter's pencil
- sewing machine (optional)

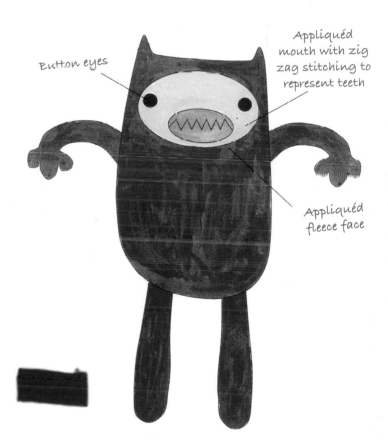

Button eyes

Appliquéd mouth with zig zag stitching to represent teeth

Appliquéd fleece face

Leo is approximately 22 cm (8¾ in) tall

TO MAKE THE MONSTER

1 Photocopy or scan the templates for making Leo on pages 112–113 and cut them out. Place the red fleece right side down on a flat surface. Position your templates and draw round them with the water-soluble pen or quilter's pencil. You will need to cut out one body shape, two leg shapes and two arm shapes. Make sure that any pile on the fabric runs down the length of the pieces in the direction of the arrows shown on the templates and remember to mark the position of the dots. You will also need to cut shapes that roughly match these pieces (for more information, see page 12), bearing in mind the direction of the pile. From the beige fleece, cut out one face shape.

2 Place the face on the body shape in the position indicated on the template, making sure that any obvious pile goes downwards, and pin or baste in position. Sew round the face using a medium zig zag stitch if your machine has this option. Alternatively, use an ordinary machine stitch or oversew in place by hand (see page 13). If you are sewing by machine, it's a good idea to start your stitching in the middle of one side of the face where the join will be least noticeable.

3 Use the template to cut out the mouth from pale pink felt and position as indicated on the template. Pin or baste in place and sew round the

mouth in matching thread using a small zig zag stitch if your machine has this option. Alternatively use a machine running stitch or oversew it in place using tiny stitches (see page 13). Work the mouth in a large machine zig zag stitch, going over your work two or three times to make the mouth stand out. Alternatively, embroider a row of zig zag stitches using three strands of black embroidery thread. If you are embroidering the mouth by hand, you may find it useful to draw a guideline first using the water-soluble pen or quilter's pencil.

shape 5 mm (¼ in) from the edge, leaving the flat end open for turning and stuffing. Trim away the excess fabric on the corresponding piece of fleece so that it matches the original arm shape. Trim the fleece particularly close to the seams round the fingers and make small snips between the fingers, taking care not to cut into the seam (this will help give the finished fingers a smooth shape). Complete the second arm and both legs in the same way. Turn the arms and legs the right way out and stuff.

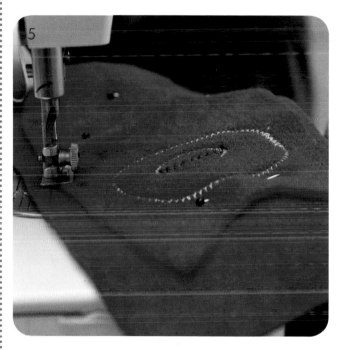

4 Place one of the arm pieces onto its corresponding piece of fleece, making sure that the right sides are together and any obvious pile on the corresponding fabric is going in the same direction as the main piece. Sew round the arm

5 Now place the body piece face down on its corresponding piece of fleece, making sure that the pieces are right sides together and any obvious pile on the corresponding fabric is going in the same direction as the main piece. Sew round the body piece 5 mm (¼ in) from the edge, leaving openings between the dots for inserting the arms and legs and for turning and stuffing. Trim away the excess fabric.

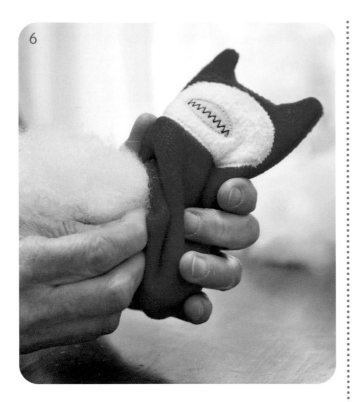

6 Turn the body the right way out and stuff. Close the opening used for turning and stuffing using slip stitch (see page 12).

7 Insert about 5 mm (¼ in) of the top of one of the arms into the opening at the side of the body. Secure by oversewing across the front and back of the arm top (see page 13). Position and secure the other arm and both legs in the same way. Using the photograph of the finished monster as a guide, sew on the two button eyes.

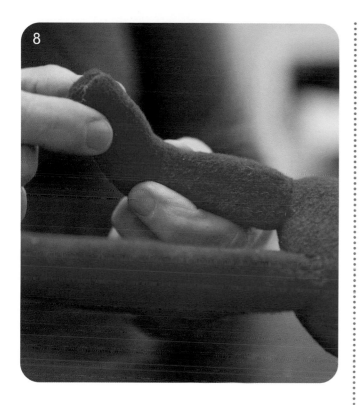

8 To make the feet, turn up 5 cm (2 in) at the end of each leg and hold in place so that the foot is at a right angle to the leg. Now, using the thread double for strength and starting at one of the side seams, work a few large, loose slip stitches (see page 12) across the curve at the front of the ankle. Pull up the thread fairly tightly and secure.

9 For the claws, use three strands of lime green embroidery thread. Secure the thread invisibly in the side seam and take the needle out through the top of the foot ready to sew the first claw. Now take the thread over the end of the foot, through the back and out through the top again, ready to work the next claw. Work two more claws the same way and secure the thread in the side seam.

*COOL IDEA

For an extra jaunty version of Leo, try sewing one arm pointing downwards and the other one pointing up.

Zoltan

A little bit dragon, a touch of chameleon and a good dash of lizard – Zoltan certainly has exotic ancestry. You'll have to try to keep on the right side of him as he can get huffy quite easily. But if you're nice to him, he's a good creature to have on your side.

** Quite easy

MATERIALS

- a piece of purple fleece measuring 25 x 42 cm (10 x 16½ in). If the fabric has an obvious pile this should run down its longer length.
- a piece of orange fleece, 5 x 20 cm (2 x 8 in) for the spikes
- a small piece of lime green fleece for the body markings
- scraps of black and white felt for the eye
- bright pink embroidery thread for the mouth
- 20 g (¾ oz) polyester toy stuffing
- matching threads for your fabrics including the felt

TOOLS

- access to a photocopier or computer with scanner and printer
- scissors
- sewing needles
- dressmaking pins
- water-soluble pen or quilter's pencil
- sewing machine (optional)

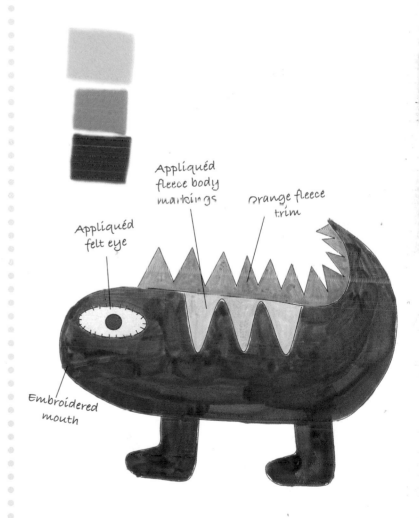

Appliquéd fleece body markings

Orange fleece trim

Appliquéd felt eye

Embroidered mouth

Zoltan is approximately 20 cm (8 in) long

TO MAKE THE MONSTER

1 Photocopy or scan the templates for making Zoltan on pages 114–115 and cut them out. Place the purple fleece right side down on a flat surface. Position your template and draw round it

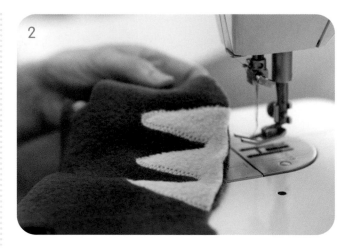

with the water-soluble pen or quilter's pencil. If you want Zoltan to face right, as in the photograph, use the template face down. If you want your creature to face left, use the template the right way up. You will need to cut out just one body shape at this stage. Make sure that any pile on the fabric runs down the length of the piece in the direction of the arrow shown on the template and remember to mark the position of the dots. You will also need to cut a shape that roughly matches the body piece (for more information, see page 12), bearing in mind the direction of the pile. Cut out the body markings shape from lime green fleece, making sure any pile runs down the length of the piece, as shown on the template.

2 Position the body markings onto the body, as indicated on the template and stitch in place. Use a small zig zag stitch if your machine has this option. Alternatively, use an ordinary machine stitch or oversew by hand (see page 13).

3 Draw round the spikes template on the reverse side of the orange fleece using the water-soluble pen or quilter's pencil but do not cut out just yet. Sew just inside the cutting line of the spikes using a small zig zag stitch if you are using a sewing machine and your machine has this facility. Alternatively, use a straight machine or hand running stitch. Trim very close to the stitching using embroidery scissors, taking care not to cut the stitching itself.

4 Lay the spikes right side down on the right side of the body shape, along the line indicated on the template at the top of the body, so that the spikes face inwards and the long, lower flat edge of the spikes lines up with the flat edge of the body. The longer spikes should be at the head end of the body. Baste the spikes in position.

5 Cut one outer eye from white felt and one inner eye from black felt. Using the template as a guide, oversew the eye pieces in place using tiny stitches (see page 13). When you have finished, gently tease round the stitches with the tip of a needle so that your stitches become almost invisible.

7 For Zoltan's mouth, work a row of small chain stitches (see page 14) using three strands of bright pink embroidery thread.

6 Now place the body piece face down on the corresponding piece of fleece, making sure that the pieces are right sides together and any obvious pile on the corresponding fabric is going in the same direction as the main piece. Sew round the body piece 5 mm (¼ in) from the edge, leaving an opening between the dots for turning and stuffing. Trim away the excess fabric. Turn the body the right way out and stuff. Close the opening used for turning and stuffing using slip stitch (see page 12).

*COOL IDEA

If you don't fancy sewing Zoltan's spikes and want to save a bit of time, try sewing small loops of ribbon along his back instead.

Rufus

He may be small but there's a lot going on in this creature's big head. He feels sure his smile will win the admiration of lady fleecie monsters everywhere and he doesn't care at all that his teeth are an orthodontist's nightmare.

✱✱ Quite easy

MATERIALS

- a piece of pale blue fleece measuring 27 x 36 cm (10½ x 14 in). If the fabric has an obvious pile this should run down its shorter length.
- a small piece of orange fleece for the horns
- a small piece of lime green fleece or felt for the eye
- scraps of black and white felt for the eye
- red and white embroidery thread for the mouth and teeth
- 20 g (¾ oz) polyester toy stuffing
- matching threads for your fabrics including the felt

TOOLS

- access to a photocopier or computer with scanner and printer
- scissors
- sewing needles
- dressmaking pins
- water-soluble pen or quilter's pencil
- sewing machine (optional)

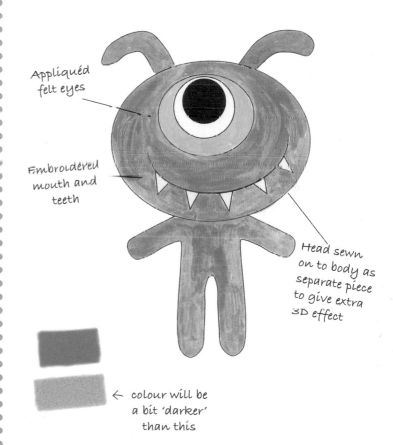

Appliquéd felt eyes

Embroidered mouth and teeth

Head sewn on to body as separate piece to give extra 3D effect

← colour will be a bit 'darker' than this

Rufus is approximately 18 cm (7 in) tall

65

TO MAKE THE MONSTER

1 Photocopy or scan the templates for making Rufus on pages 116–117 and cut them out. Place the pale blue fleece right side down on a flat surface. Position your templates and draw round them with the water-soluble pen or quilter's pencil, remembering to mark the position of the dots. You will need to cut out one head shape and one body shape. For the body shape, make sure that any pile on the fabric runs down the length of the piece in the direction of the arrows shown on the template. You will also need to cut shapes that roughly match these pieces (for more information, see page 12), bearing in mind the direction of the pile. From the orange fleece, cut out two horn shapes and two shapes that roughly match them. Cut out one outer eye piece from the lime green fleece or felt, one middle eye piece from the white felt and one inner eye piece from the black felt.

2 Position the lime green fleece or felt outer eye on the face, as indicated on the template, making sure that the pile on the head is going down its length. Pin or baste in place and sew round it using a machine or hand running stitch. Using the template as a guide, oversew the outer and inner eye pieces in place (see page 13). When you have finished, gently tease round the stitches with the tip of a needle so that the stitches become almost invisible.

3 Using three strands of red embroidery thread, embroider the mouth using chain stitch (see page 14). Before you begin, you may find it useful to draw a line using the water-soluble pen or quilter's pencil as a guide. Stitch the teeth by working six individual chain stitches (see page 14) just below the mouth, using the photograph as a guide.

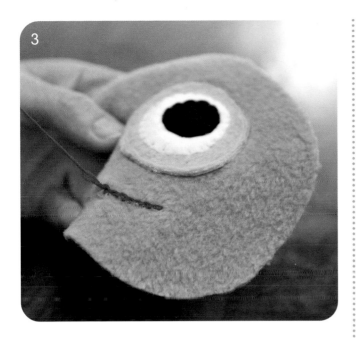

end open for turning. Trim away the excess fabric on the corresponding piece of fleece so that it matches the original horn shape. Complete the second horn in the same way then turn the horns the right way out but do not stuff.

5 Position the horns on the face where indicated on the template so that the horns lie down the length of the face, so that the curved ends point outwards and the raw edges line up with the raw edge of the head. Baste in position.

4 Place one of the horn pieces onto its corresponding piece of fleece, making sure that the right sides are together and any obvious pile on the corresponding fabric is going in the same direction as the main piece. Sew round the horn shape 5 mm (¼ in) in from the edge, leaving the flat

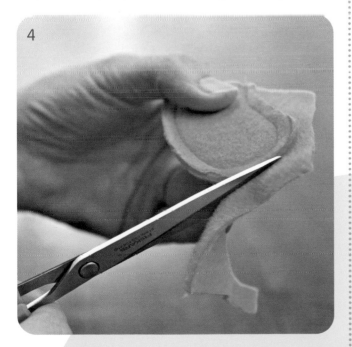

6 Place the head piece face down on the corresponding piece of fleece making sure that the two pieces of fabric are right sides together and that any obvious pile on the corresponding fabric is going in the same direction as the main piece. Stitch round the shape 5 mm (¼ in) from the edge, leaving an opening between the dots for turning and stuffing. Trim away the excess fabric. Turn the head the right way out, stuff and then slip stitch the opening closed (see page 12).

7 Fold the body piece in half lengthways so that the fleecie side of the fabric is on the inside. Sew the body dart – from the neck down to the tummy – using a small running stitch or medium length machine stitch.

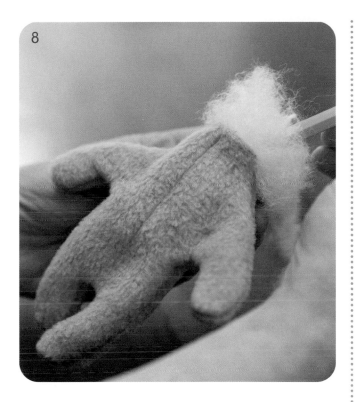

8

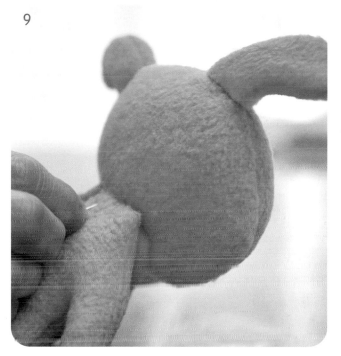

9 To join the head to the body, tuck the raw edges of the neck inwards and slip stitch the opening closed (see page 12). Oversew the neck to the centre of the back of the head, just below half way down. Turn the creature over and slip stitch the underside of the chin to the front of the chest to secure the head in position.

9

8 Now place the body piece face down on its corresponding piece of fleece, making sure that the pieces are right sides together and any obvious pile on the corresponding fabric is going in the same direction as the main piece. Sew round the body piece 5 mm (¼ in) from the edge, leaving it open at the neck edge for turning and stuffing. Trim away the excess fabric then turn the body the right way out and stuff.

*COOL IDEA

For an almost infinite variety of Rufus-like creatures, experiment with different eyes and mouths using some of the ideas given for other projects.

With the quirky appeal of a strange species of duck, Albert is the perfect fleecie monster for bird lovers everywhere. With his smart striped breast and curvy yellow wings, he stands tall and proud. Best of all, he will never utter a single annoying quack.

Albert

✳✳✳ Some sewing experience useful

MATERIALS

- a piece of orange fleece measuring 16 x 28 cm (6¼ x 11 in). If the fabric has an obvious pile this should run down its shorter length.
- a piece of yellow fleece measuring 28 x 14 cm (11 x 5½ in). If the fabric has an obvious pile this should run down its shorter length.
- a small piece of red fleece
- a small piece of multicolour striped fleece for the breast
- a scrap of lime green fleece or felt for the eye
- two odd buttons for the eyes – one about 17 mm (¾ in) diameter and the other about 11 mm (½ in) diameter
- 30 g (1 oz) polyester toy stuffing
- matching threads for your fabrics (except for the lime fleece or felt for the eye)

TOOLS

- access to a photocopier or computer with scanner and printer
- scissors
- sewing needles
- dressmaking pins
- water-soluble pen or quilter's pencil
- sewing machine (optional)

Buttons on felt base

Overstitched fleece wings

Appliqué fabric patch

possible fabric for patch

Albert is approximately 26 cm (10¼ in) tall

TO MAKE THE MONSTER

1 Photocopy or scan the templates for making Albert on pages 118–119 and cut them out. Place the orange fleece right side down on a flat surface. Position your body template and draw round it with the water-soluble pen or quilter's pencil. You will need to cut out two body shapes from the orange fleece. Make sure that any pile on the fabric runs down the length of the pieces in the direction of the arrows shown on the templates and

remember to mark the position of the dots. From the red fleece, cut out two face pieces – one using the template the right way up and one using it face down. From the striped fleece, cut out one tummy patch. From the yellow fleece, cut out two leg, two wing and two beak pieces. You will also need to cut shapes that roughly match the two leg and wing pieces (for more information, see page 12), bearing in mind the direction of the pile.

2 Place the two wing pieces face up on the wrong side of the corresponding pieces of

yellow fleece, making sure that any pile is going in the same direction on all pieces. Using a machine or hand running stitch, sew round the wings about 5 mm (¼ in) from the edge, leaving the flat edge open. Trim away the excess fabric on the corresponding pieces of fleece so that they match the original wing shapes.

3 Place one of the leg shapes onto its corresponding piece of fleece, making sure that the right sides are together and any obvious pile on

the corresponding fabric is going in the same direction as the main piece. Sew round the leg shape 5 mm (¼ in) from the edge, leaving the top end open for turning and stuffing. Trim away the excess fabric on the corresponding piece of fleece so that it matches the original leg shape. Complete the second leg in the same way. Turn the legs the right way out and stuff.

4 Place the tummy patch in the centre of one of the body pieces, making sure that any obvious pile goes downwards, and pin or baste in position. Sew round the patch using a small zig zag stitch if your machine has this option. Alternatively, use an ordinary machine stitch or oversew by hand (see page 13). Place the beak pieces right side down on the face pieces so that the flat edges line up and the beak points towards the back of the head. Seam together leaving a 5-mm (¼-in) seam allowance. If you want Albert to face right, as shown in the photo, position the green outer eye on the head piece with the beak pointing right, using the position guide shown on the template. If you want

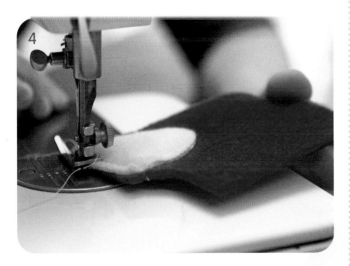

Albert facing left, sew his eye to the head piece with the beak pointing left. Sew in place using a machine or hand running stitch and red thread.

5 Seam the two head pieces to the two body pieces in matching threads, remembering to seam the head shape with the eye piece to the body shape with the tummy patch and leaving a 5-mm (¼-in) seam allowance. Remember to leave an opening between the dots for turning and stuffing

on the pieces that will form the reverse of the creature, as indicated on the template.

6 Position the wings along the sides of the creature, as shown on the template, so that the curved sections point inwards and the raw edges of the wings line up with the raw edges of the body. Baste in position. Place the two creature shapes right sides together, checking that the neck and beak seams line up, and stitch round the complete creature in matching threads, 5 mm (¼ in) from the edge, leaving openings between the dots for inserting the legs. Turn the right way out through the gap at the back of the neck. Stuff then slip stitch the opening closed (see page 12).

7 Insert about 5 mm (¼ in) of the top of one of the legs into the opening at the bottom of the body. Secure by oversewing across the front and back of the leg top (see page 13). Position and secure the other leg in the same way.

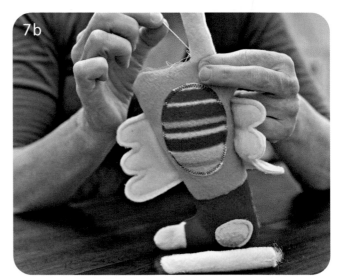

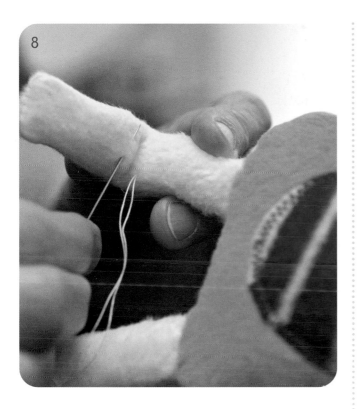

9 Complete Albert by sewing the two buttons in place, one on top of the other, as shown in the photograph.

8 To make the feet, turn up 4 cm (1½ in) at the end of each leg and hold in place so that the foot is at a right angle to the leg. Now, using your thread double for strength and starting at one of the side seams, work a few large, loose slip stitches (see page 12) across the curve at the front of the ankle. Pull up the thread fairly tightly and secure.

*COOL IDEA

To make Albert really funky, try designing your own cockerel comb that can be seamed into his head.

Dotty

With her pearly flower eyes and bright pink lips, Dotty truly believes she's the personification of feminine charm. She's as proud as it's possible to be of her pink spotty coat and her extra-long arms make it impossible for other creatures to escape her amorous embraces.

** Quite easy

MATERIALS

- a piece of spotted pink fleece measuring 60 x 29 cm (23½ x 11½). If the fabric has an obvious pile this should run down its shorter length.
- a scrap of bright pink fleece for the lips
- two white flower-shape buttons approximately 13 mm (½ in) diameter and two black buttons approximately 18 mm (¾ in) diameter for the eyes
- 35 g (1¼ oz) polyester toy stuffing
- matching threads for your fabrics, plus dark grey thread for the mouth

TOOLS

- access to a photocopier or computer with scanner and printer
- scissors
- sewing needles
- dressmaking pins
- water-soluble pen or quilter's pencil
- sewing machine (optional)

fancy button eyes

padded effect on fleece mouth

This fleece has big coloured spots

Dotty is approximately 33 cm (13 in) tall

TO MAKE THE MONSTER

1 Photocopy or scan the templates for making Dotty on pages 120–121 and cut them out. Place the spotted fleece right side down on a flat surface. Position your templates and draw round them with the water-soluble pen or quilter's pencil. You will need to cut out one body shape, two arm and two leg shapes. Make sure that any pile on the fabric

runs down the length of the pieces in the direction of the arrows shown on the templates and remember to mark the position of the dots. You will also need to cut shapes that roughly match these pieces (for more information, see page 12), bearing in mind the direction of the pile. From the bright pink fleece, cut out one lip shape.

2 Position the lip shape on the body shape, as indicated on the template with the pile running down the piece, as on the body, and oversew round the edge (see page 13). When you are about 2 cm (¾ in) from completing the oversewing, insert a small piece of stuffing into the lips to give them a slightly padded look, before completing your stitching. Now, if sewing by machine, work two

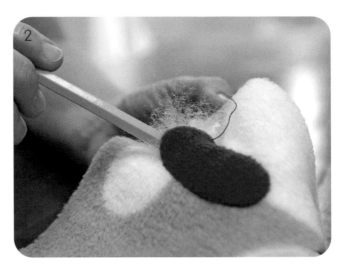

rows of running stitch, one on top the other, across and just to the outside of the lips, using dark grey thread. If you are sewing by hand, use your thread double and work a row of back stitch (see page 14). If you like, draw a guideline across the lips using the water-soluble pen or quilter's pencil before you start stitching.

3 Place one of the arm pieces onto its corresponding piece of fleece, making sure that the right sides are together and any obvious pile on the corresponding fabric is going in the same direction as the main piece. Sew round the arm shape 5 mm (¼ in) from the edge, leaving the flat end open for turning and stuffing. Trim away the

excess fabric on the corresponding piece of fleece so that it matches the original arm shape. Complete the second arm and both legs in the same way. Turn the limbs the right way out and stuff.

4 Now place the body piece face down on its corresponding piece of fleece, making sure that the pieces are right sides together and any obvious pile on the corresponding fabric is going in the same

direction as the main piece. Sew round the body piece 5 mm (¼ in) from the edge, leaving openings between the dots for inserting the arms and legs, and for turning and stuffing. Trim away the excess fabric to match the body shape. Turn the body the right way out and stuff. Close the opening used for turning and stuffing using slip stitch (see page 12).

5 Insert about 5 mm (¼ in) of the top of one of the arms into the opening at the side of the body. Secure by oversewing across the front and back of the arm top (see page 13). Position and secure the other arm and both legs in the same way.

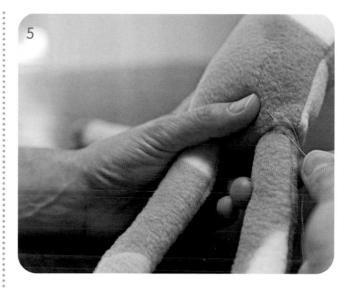

6 Complete Dotty by sewing the buttons in place, one on top of the other, as shown in the photograph.

*COOL IDEA

Why not make Dotty her very own boyfriend using a bright coloured spotted fleece and star buttons instead of flower buttons for his eyes?

Beatrice

Skittish Beatrice, with her lime green coat and wonky teeth, is proud of her feline heritage. In her brightly coloured skirt, she's a dedicated follower of fashion. And while she's a good friend to those she loves – she can be just a little bit touchy.

✱✱ Quite easy

MATERIALS

- a piece of green fleece measuring 23 x 46 cm (9 x 18 in). If the fabric has an obvious pile this should run down its shorter length.
- a scrap of yellow fleece for the eye patch
- a scrap of bright pink felt for the mouth
- two odd buttons for the eyes
- a 39 x 12 cm (15½ x 4¾ in) piece of patterned cotton fabric for the skirt
- a 41-cm (16¼-in) length of narrow pink ric rac tape for the skirt trim
- an 18-cm (7 in) length of narrow elastic or elastic cord for the skirt waistband
- matching threads for your fabrics and ric rac
- black sewing thread for the teeth (or black embroidery thread if you want to sew by hand)
- bright pink embroidery thread for the claws
- 30 g (1 oz) polyester toy stuffing

TOOLS

- access to a photocopier or computer with scanner and printer
- scissors
- sewing needles
- dressmaking pins and a small safety pin
- water-soluble pen or quilter's pencil
- sewing machine (optional)
- iron

zingy cotton print for the skirt

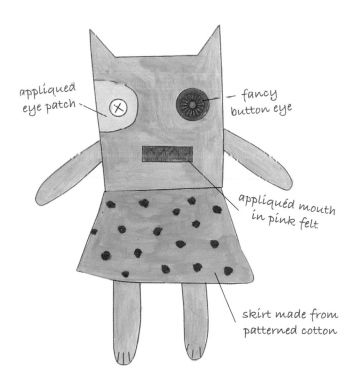

appliquéd eye patch

fancy button eye

appliquéd mouth in pink felt

skirt made from patterned cotton

Beatrice is approximately 33 cm (13 in) tall

TO MAKE THE MONSTER

1 Photocopy or scan the templates for making Beatrice on pages 122–123 and cut them out. Place the green fleece right side down on a flat surface. Position your templates and draw round them with the water-soluble pen or quilter's pencil. You will need to cut out one body shape, two arm

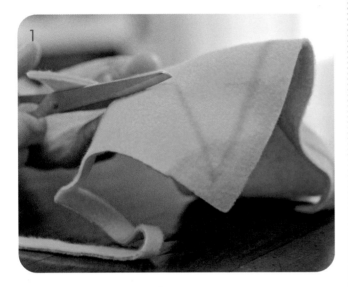

and two leg shapes. Make sure that any pile on the fabric runs down the length of the pieces in the direction of the arrows shown on the templates and remember to mark the position of the dots. You will also need to cut shapes that roughly match these pieces (for more information, see page 12), bearing in mind the direction of the pile. From the yellow fleece, cut out one eye patch and cut out one mouth from the bright pink felt.

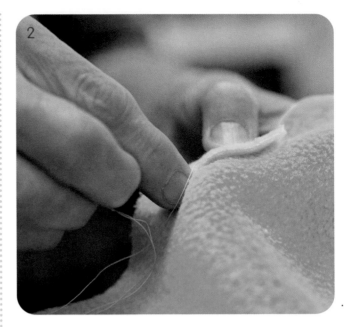

2 Place the eye patch on the head as shown on the template, making sure that any obvious pile goes downwards, and pin or baste. Oversew the patch in position (see page 13).

3 Position the mouth as shown on the template and oversew in place. Using the water-soluble pen or quilter's pencil, draw the zig zag for the

teeth. If you are sewing by machine, work two rows of running stitch in black thread, one on top the other, along the zig zag line. If you are sewing by hand, work along the line in back stitch (see page 14) using three strands of black embroidery thread.

4 Place one of the arm pieces onto its corresponding piece of fleece, making sure that the right sides are together and any obvious pile on the corresponding fabric is going in the same direction as the main piece. Sew round the arm shape 5 mm (¼ in) from the edge, leaving the flat end open for turning and stuffing. Trim away the excess fabric on the corresponding piece of fleece so that it matches the original arm shape. Complete the second arm and both legs in the same way. Turn the limbs the right way out and stuff.

5 Now place the body piece face down on its corresponding piece of fleece, making sure that the pieces are right sides together and any obvious pile on the corresponding fabric is going in the same direction as the main piece. Sew round the body piece 5 mm (¼ in) from the edge, leaving openings between the dots for inserting the arms and legs, and for turning and stuffing. Clip off the tips of the ears, close to the stitching (this will help make the ears pointy). Turn the body the right way out and stuff. Close the opening used for turning and stuffing using slip stitch (see page 12).

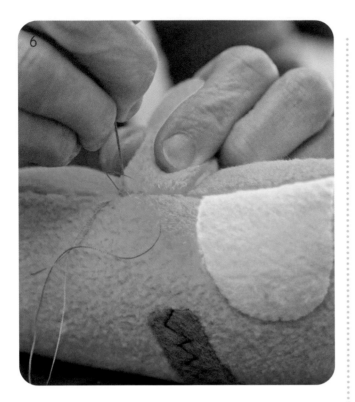

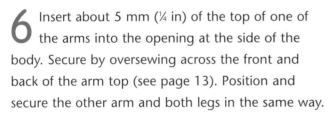

6 Insert about 5 mm (¼ in) of the top of one of the arms into the opening at the side of the body. Secure by oversewing across the front and back of the arm top (see page 13). Position and secure the other arm and both legs in the same way.

7 For the claws, use three strands of pink embroidery thread. Secure the thread invisibly in the side seam and take the needle out through the top of the foot, ready to sew the first claw. Now take the thread over the end of the foot, through the back and out through the top again, ready to work the next claw. Work two more claws in the same way and secure the thread in the side seam. Repeat for the other foot. To complete Beatrice, sew on the two button eyes.

FOR THE SKIRT

1 Fold the rectangle in half widthways so that the pattern is on the inside, and stitch the back seam leaving a 5-mm (¼-in) seam allowance. Press the seam open. For the hem, turn under 1 cm (⅜ in) at

the bottom edge and press in place. Turn up another 1 cm (⅜ in) and press again. Stitch close to the folded edge using a machine running stitch or hand hemming stitch (see page 13). Position the ric rac tape along the lower edge about 1 cm (⅜ in) from the bottom. Stitch in place by hand or machine along the centre of the tape.

2 For the waistband casing, prepare the fabric as for the hem but, when sewing, leave a 1-cm (⅜-in) opening at the back seam for threading the elastic. Using the small safety pin, thread the elastic through the casing. Adjust the elastic so that the skirt will fit securely round the creature's waist and trim if necessary. Overlap the ends of the elastic and stitch together securely – or knot the ends together tightly.

✳COOL IDEA

You can give Beatrice a variety of expressions, depending on the buttons you choose for her eyes. Take a bit of time to choose ones that you really like.

Three Mini Monsters

Wilf, Prudence and Melvin are three cute little guys that you can fit in your pocket. Now, you'll never need to be without a fleecie monster, wherever you are!

* Really easy

MATERIALS

Wilf

- a piece of lime green fleece measuring 28 x 16 cm (11 x 6¼ in). If the fabric has an obvious pile this should run down its shorter length.
- a scrap of dark grey felt for the eyes
- a scrap of pale pink felt for the mouth
- white embroidery thread for the teeth
- bright pink embroidery thread for the eye
- 15 g (½ oz) polyester toy stuffing
- matching threads for your fabrics

Prudence

- a piece of bright pink fleece measuring 34 x 16 cm (13½ x 6¼ in). If the fabric has an obvious pile this should run down its shorter length.
- a scrap of yellow fleece for the face panel
- a scrap of black felt for the eyes
- orange embroidery thread for the mouth
- 15 g (½ oz) polyester toy stuffing
- matching threads for your fabrics

Melvin

- a piece of orange fleece measuring 28 x 16 cm (11 x 6¼ in) (if the fabric has an obvious pile this should run down the shorter length of the fabric)
- an odd cream button for one of the eyes
- turquoise embroidery thread for the other eye
- dark grey embroidery thread for the mouth
- a scrap of white felt for the teeth
- 15 g (½ oz) polyester toy stuffing
- matching threads for your fabrics

TOOLS

- access to a photocopier or computer with scanner and printer
- scissors
- sewing needles
- dressmaking pins
- water-soluble pen or quilter's pencil
- sewing machine (optional)

Wilf, Prudence and Melvin are approximately 13 cm (5¼ in) tall

FOR WILF

1 Photocopy or scan the templates for making Wilf on page 125 and cut them out. Place the lime green fleece right side down on a flat surface. Position your template and draw round it with the water-soluble pen or quilter's pencil. You will need to cut out one body shape only at this stage. Make

sure that any pile on the fabric runs down the length of the piece in the direction of the arrow shown on the template and remember to mark the position of the dots. You will also need to cut a shape that roughly matches the body piece (for more information, see page 12), bearing in mind the direction of the pile. Cut out the mouth shape from pale pink and the eyes from the dark grey felt.

2 Place the mouth in position, as shown on the template and oversew in place using tiny stitches (see page 13). Position and sew the eyes in the same way. Gently tease round the stitches with the tip of your needle so that the stitches become almost invisible.

3 Embroider the teeth with six strands of white embroidery thread, using single chain stitch (see page 14). With six strands of bright pink embroidery thread and large running stitches, work a star shape over the larger eye.

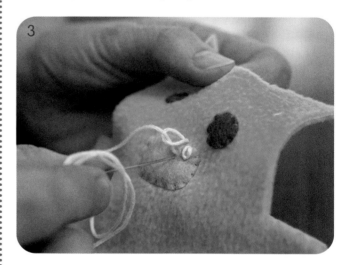

4 Now place the body piece face down on its corresponding piece of fleece, making sure that the pieces are right sides together and any obvious pile on the corresponding fabric is going in the same direction as the main piece. Sew round the body piece 5 mm (¼ in) from the edge, leaving an

opening between the dots for turning and stuffing. Trim away the excess fabric to match the body shape. Turn the body the right way out and stuff. Close the opening used for turning and stuffing using slip stitch (see page 12).

FOR PRUDENCE

1 Photocopy or scan the templates for making Prudence on page 124 and cut them out. Place the bright pink fleece right side down on a flat surface. Position your template and draw round it with the water-soluble pen or quilter's pencil. You will need to cut out one body shape only at this stage. Make sure that any pile on the fabric runs down the length of the piece in the direction of the arrow shown on the template and remember to mark the position of the dots. You will also need to cut a shape that roughly matches the body piece (for more information, see page 12), bearing in mind the direction of the pile. Cut out the face from yellow fleece and the eyes from the black felt.

2 Place the face panel on the head as shown on the template, making sure that any obvious pile goes downwards, and pin or baste in position. Sew round the face using a small zig zag stitch if your machine has this option. Alternatively, use an ordinary machine stitch or oversew by hand (see page 13).

3 Embroider the mouth in back stitch (see page 14) using six strands of orange embroidery thread. Position the eyes and oversew in

place using tiny stitches (see page 13). Gently tease round the stitches with the tip of a needle so they become almost invisible.

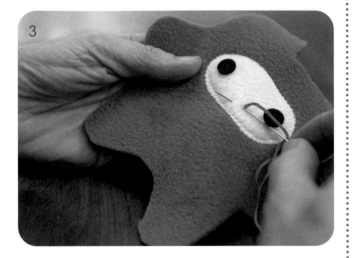

4 Now place the body piece face down on the corresponding piece of fleece, making sure that the pieces are right sides together and any obvious pile on the corresponding fabric is going in the same direction as the main piece. Sew round the body piece 5 mm (¼ in) from the edge, leaving an opening between the dots for turning and stuffing. Trim away the excess fabric. Turn the body the right way out and stuff. Close the opening used for turning and stuffing using slip stitch (see page 12).

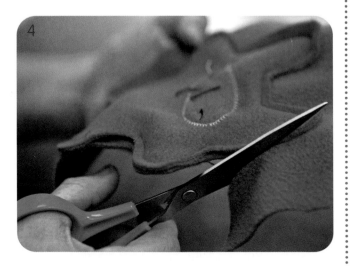

5 Squeeze the base of the ears inwards and secure the pleat with a couple of stitches.

FOR MELVIN

1 Photocopy or scan the template for making Melvin on page 125 and cut it out. Place the orange fleece right side down on a flat surface. Position your template and draw round it with the

water-soluble pen or quilter's pencil. You will need to cut out one body shape only at this stage. Make sure that any pile on the fabric runs down the length of the piece in the direction of the arrow shown on the template and remember to mark the position of the dots. You will also need to cut a shape that roughly matches the body piece (for more information, see page 12), bearing in mind the direction of the pile.

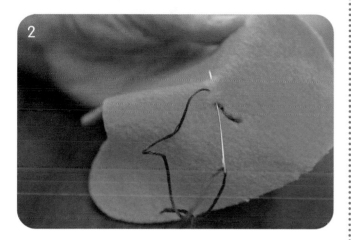

2 Using the template as a guide, embroider the mouth in chain stitch or back stitch using six strands of dark grey embroidery thread (see page 14). You might find it helpful to draw the mouth shape with the water-soluble pen or quilter's pencil before you begin stitching.

3 Cut two small rectangles of white felt for the teeth. Using the template as a guide, oversew in place using tiny stitches (see page 13). Gently tease round the stitches with the tip of a needle. Work a single cross stitch for the right-hand eye

using six strands of turquoise embroidery thread and sew on the button for the second eye.

4 Now place the body piece face down on its corresponding piece of fleece, making sure that the pieces are right sides together and any obvious pile is going in the same direction as the main piece. Sew round the body piece 5 mm (¼ in) from the edge, leaving an opening between the dots for turning and stuffing. Trim away the excess fabric to match the body shape. Turn the body the right way out and stuff. Close the opening used for turning and stuffing using slip stitch (see page 12). Sew on the button for Melvin's second eye.

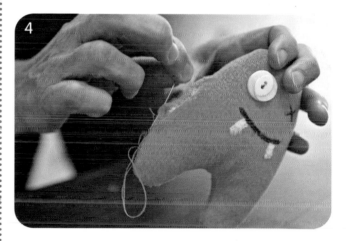

*COOL IDEA

Sew a short length of ribbon into the top seam when stitching the mini monsters together. Use your hanging mini monster to make a big funky key ring or a hanging decoration for a doorknob.

Starry-eyed Monty with his winning smile and cheerful spots looks as if he's just dropped in from Planet Happy. If he could laugh, it would be a sort of tingling giggle that never stops. If you want to put a zing in your step and lift your mood, then Monty is definitely the fleecie monster for you.

✱✱ Quite easy

MATERIALS

- a piece spotty pale green fleece measuring 26 x 45 cm (10¼ x 17¾ in). If the fabric has an obvious pile this should run down its shorter length.
- a small piece of pale blue fleece for the face
- a scrap of bright pink felt for the eyes
- two white buttons approximately 13 mm (½ in) diameter for the eyes
- orange embroidery thread for the mouth
- 30 g (1 oz) polyester toy stuffing
- matching threads for your fabrics (except the bright pink felt)

TOOLS

- access to a photocopier or computer with scanner and printer
- scissors
- sewing needles
- dressmaking pins
- water-soluble pen or quilter's pencil
- sewing machine (optional)

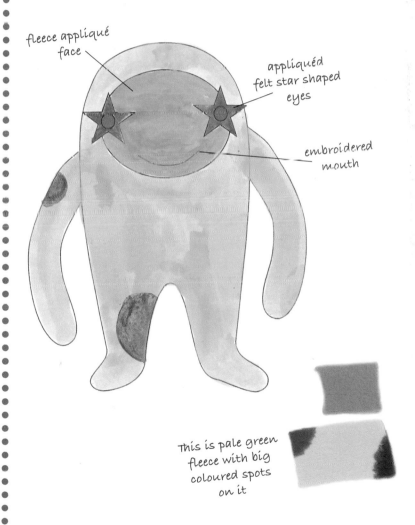

fleece appliqué face

appliquéd felt star shaped eyes

embroidered mouth

This is pale green fleece with big coloured spots on it

Monty is approximately 22 cm (8¾ in) tall

TO MAKE THE MONSTER

1 Photocopy or scan the templates for making Monty on pages 126–127 and cut them out. Place the spotty pale green fleece right side down on a flat surface. Position your templates and draw round them with the water-soluble pen or quilter's pencil. You will need to cut out one body shape and two arm shapes. Make sure that any pile on the fabric runs down the length of the pieces in the direction of the arrows shown on the templates and remember to mark the position of the dots. You will also need to cut shapes that roughly match these pieces (for more information, see page 12), bearing in mind the direction of the pile. From the pale blue fleece, cut out one face panel.

2 Place the face panel on the head as shown on the template, making sure that any obvious pile goes downwards, and pin or baste in position. Sew round the face using a small zig zag stitch if your machine has this option. Alternatively, use an ordinary machine stitch or oversew by hand (see page 13). If you are sewing by machine, it's a good idea to start your stitching in the middle of one side of the face so that any join will be hidden by the felt star eye.

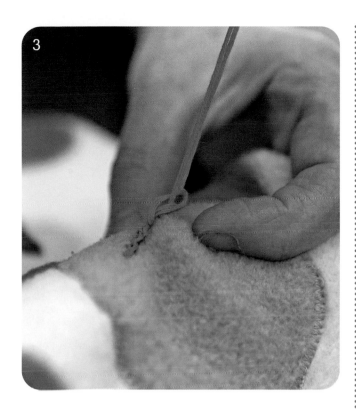

4 Place one of the arm pieces onto its corresponding piece of fleece, making sure that the right sides are together and any obvious pile on the corresponding fabric is going in the same direction as the main piece. Sew round the arm shape 5 mm (¼ in) from the edge, leaving the flat end open for turning and stuffing. Trim away the excess fabric on the corresponding piece of fleece so that it matches the original arm shape. Complete the second arm in the same way. Turn the arms the right way out and stuff.

3 Using the water soluble pen or quilter's pencil, draw the mouth onto the face panel using the template as a guide. Embroider the mouth in chain stitch (see page 14) using six strands of orange embroidery thread.

5 Now place the body piece face down on a corresponding piece of fleece, making sure that the pieces are right sides together and any obvious pile on the corresponding fabric is going in the same direction as the main piece. Sew round the body piece 5 mm (¼ in) from the edge, leaving openings between the dots for inserting the arms and for turning and stuffing. Trim away the excess fabric. Turn the body the right way out and stuff. Close the opening used for turning and stuffing using slip stitch (see page 12).

6 Insert about 5 mm (¼ in) of the top of one of the arms into the opening at the side of the body. Secure by oversewing across the front and back of the arm top (see page 13). Position and secure the other arm in the same way.

8 Using the template, cut out two star shapes from bright pink felt using small embroidery scissors. Using the photograph of the finished creature as a guide, position the star eyes and secure using the white buttons and contrasting sewing thread.

7 To make the feet, turn up 5 cm (2 in) at the end of each leg and hold in place so that the foot is at a right angle to the leg. Now, using the thread double for strength and starting at one of the side seams, work a few large, loose slip stitches (see page 12) across the curve at the front of the ankle. Pull up the thread fairly tightly and secure.

✱COOL IDEA

To make an utterly girly version of Monty, use a flower patterned fleece and the flower eyes given for Dilly and Dinah.

Toby
(see pages 16–21)

Leg (cut 2)

direction of pile

Note: all seam allowances to be 5 mm (¼ in) from edge

Arm (cut 2*)

direction of pile

* cut 1 using template face up and the other using template face down

Ear
(cut 2)

direction of pile

Face (cut 1 as appliqué)

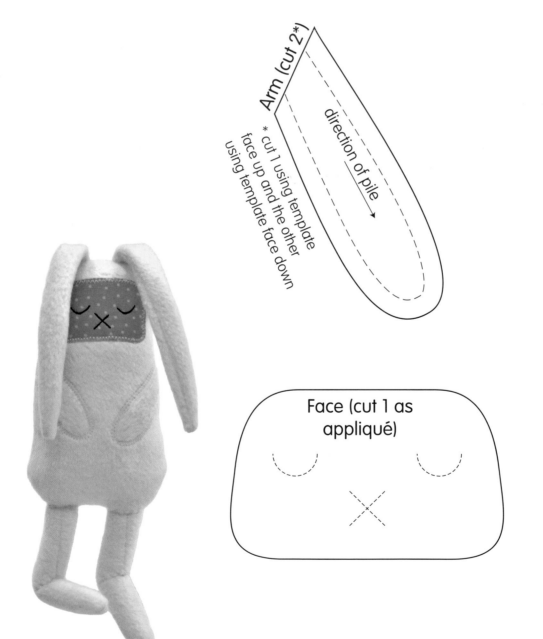

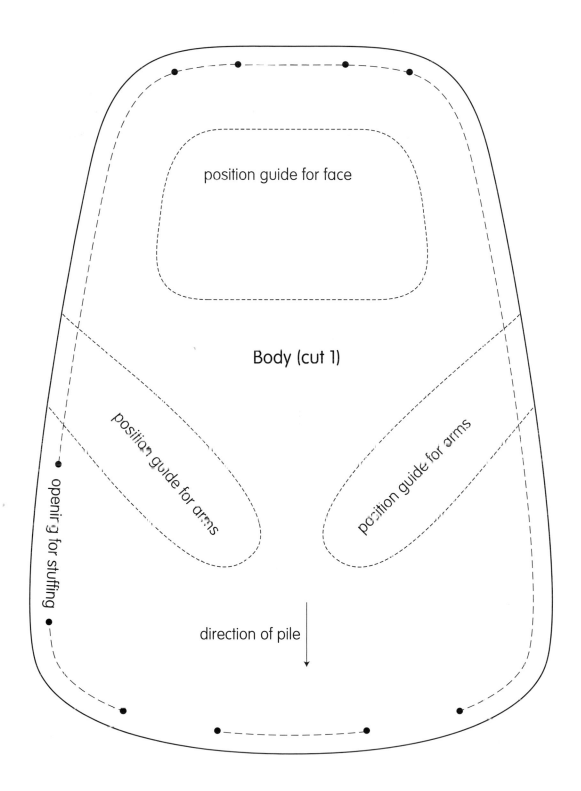

position guide for face

Body (cut 1)

position guide for arms

position guide for arms

opening for stuffing

direction of pile

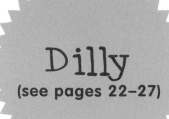

Dilly
(see pages 22–27)

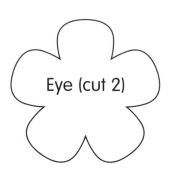

Eye (cut 2)

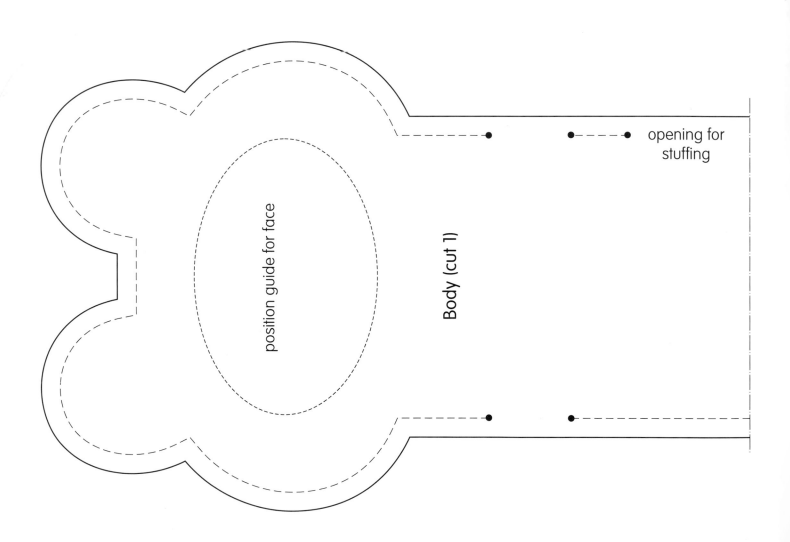

position guide for face

Body (cut 1)

opening for
stuffing

100

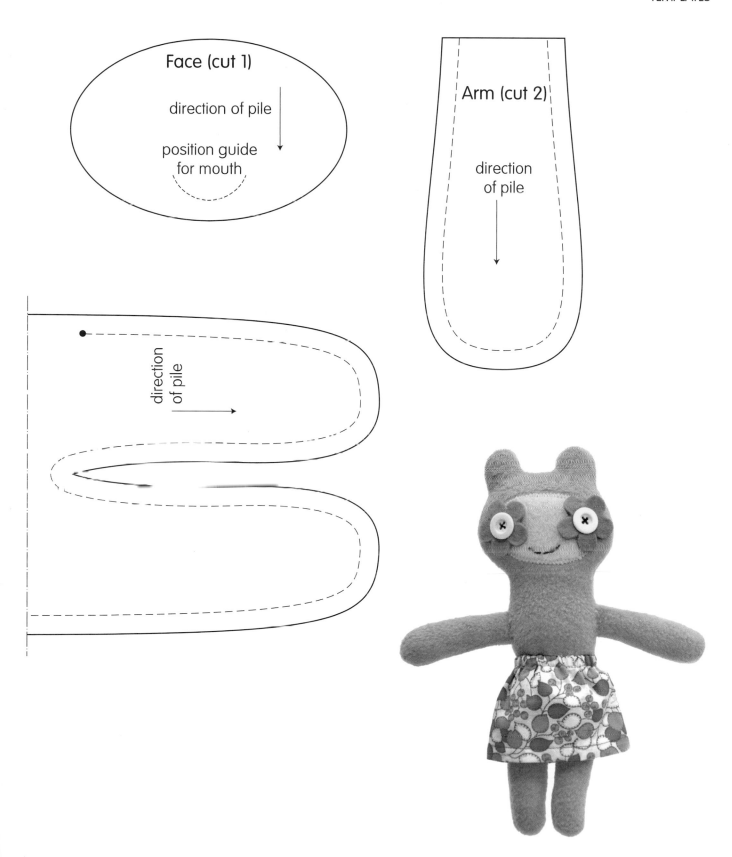

Face (cut 1)

direction of pile

position guide
for mouth

Arm (cut 2)

direction
of pile

direction
of pile

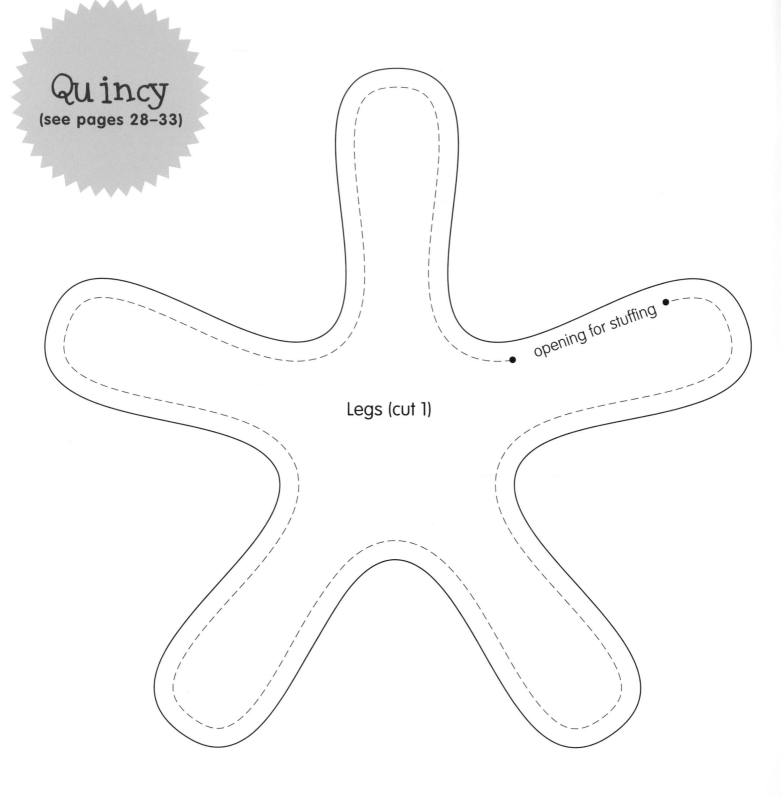

Quincy
(see pages 28–33)

opening for stuffing

Legs (cut 1)

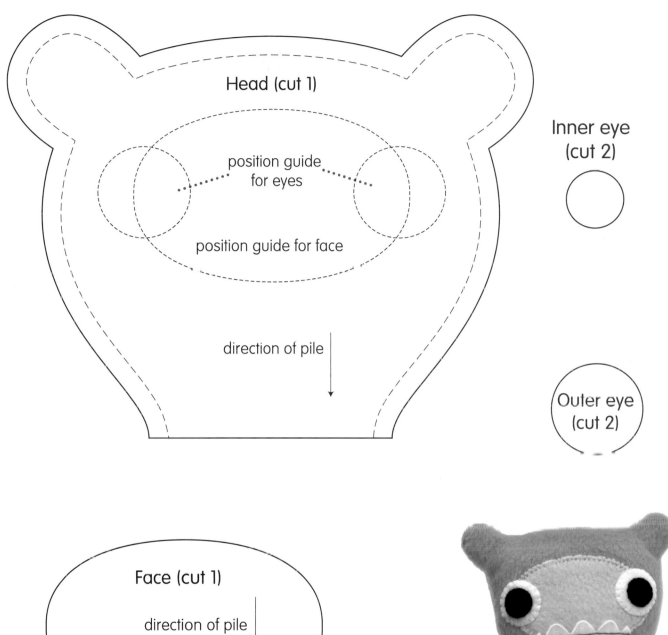

Head (cut 1)

Inner eye
(cut 2)

position guide
for eyes

position guide for face

direction of pile

Outer eye
(cut 2)

Face (cut 1)

direction of pile

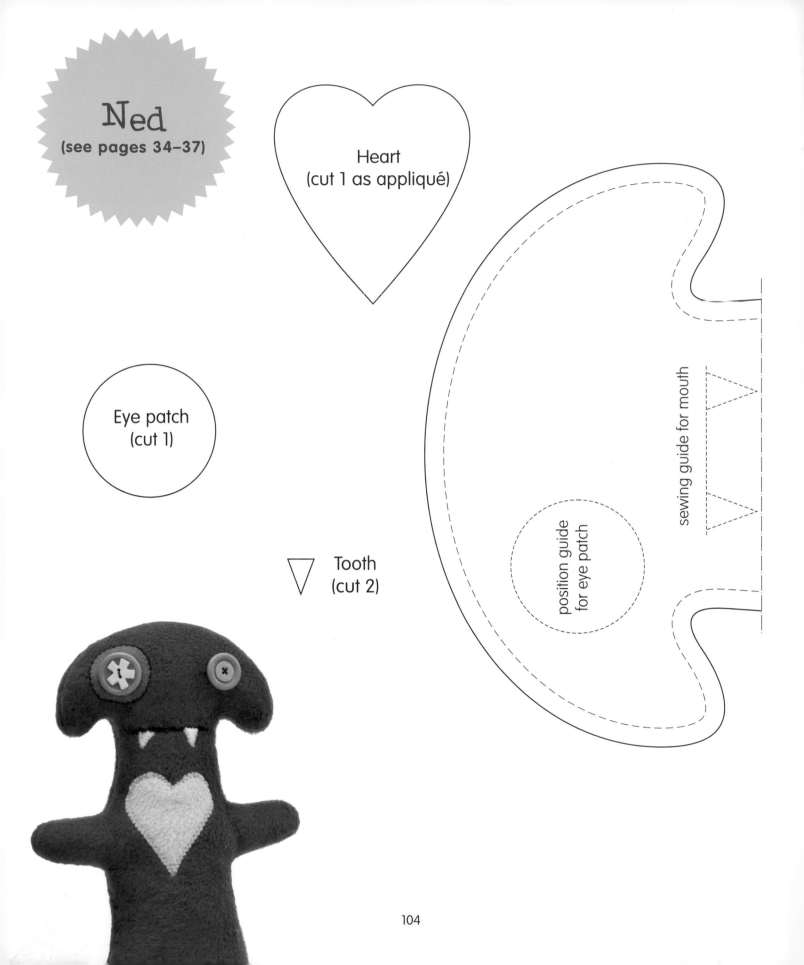

Ned
(see pages 34–37)

Heart
(cut 1 as appliqué)

Eye patch
(cut 1)

Tooth
(cut 2)

sewing guide for mouth

position guide
for eye patch

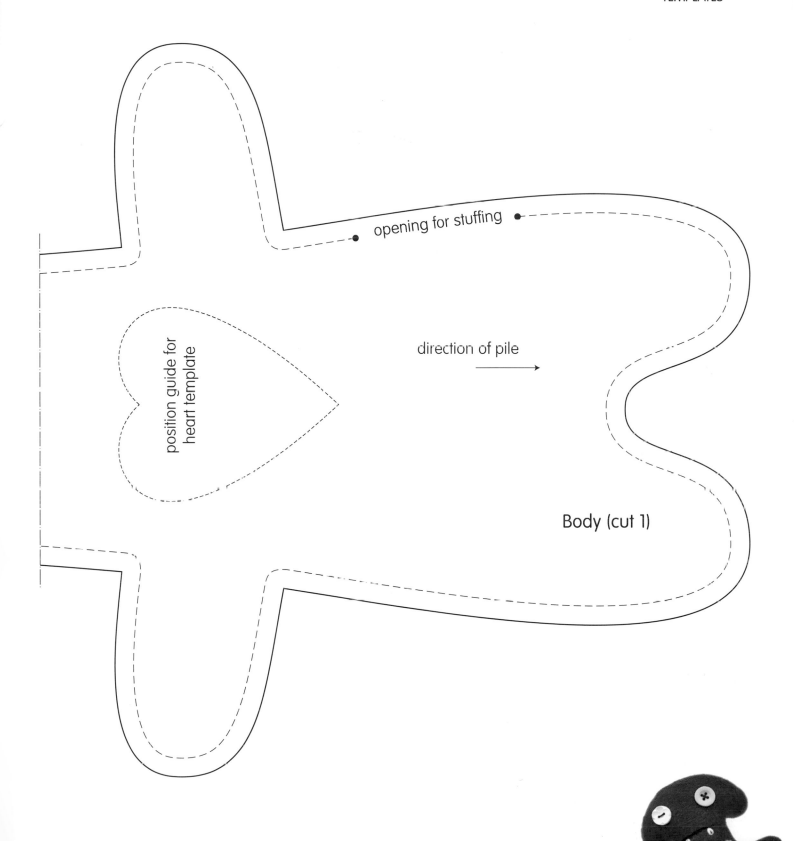

opening for stuffing

direction of pile

position guide for heart template

Body (cut 1)

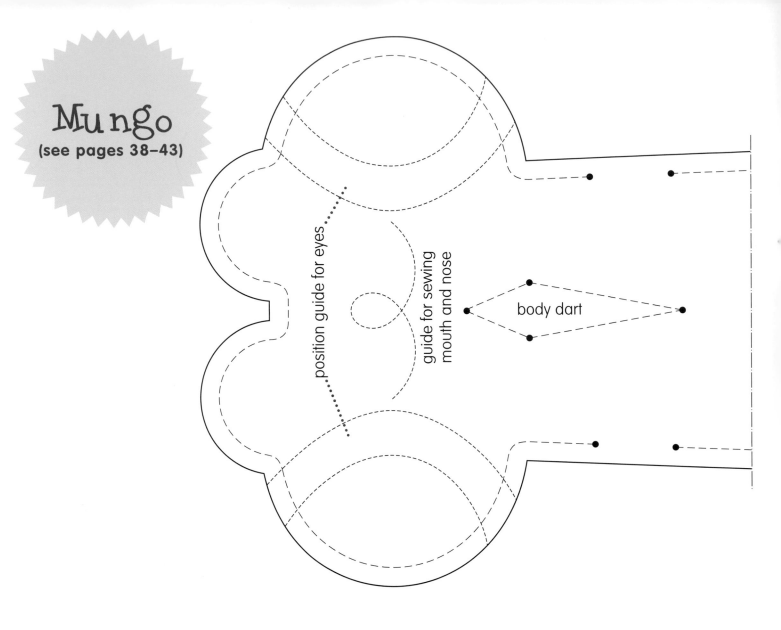

Mungo
(see pages 38–43)

position guide for eyes

guide for sewing mouth and nose

body dart

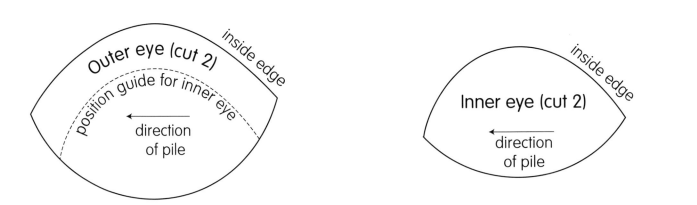

Outer eye (cut 2)

inside edge

position guide for inner eye

direction of pile

Inner eye (cut 2)

inside edge

direction of pile

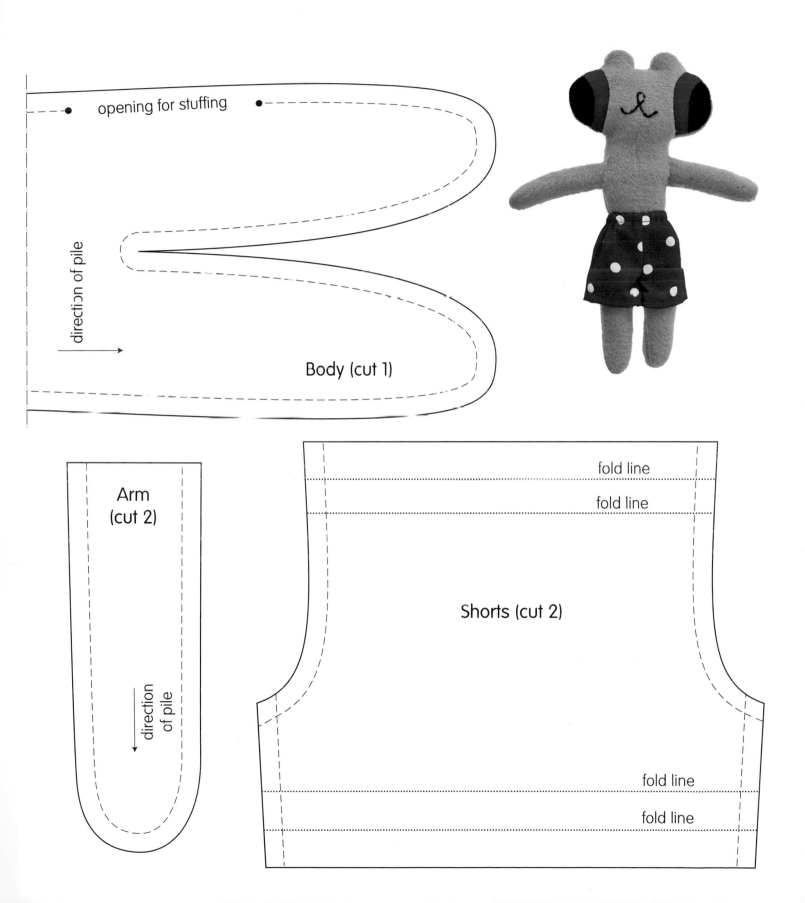

opening for stuffing

direction of pile

Body (cut 1)

Arm
(cut 2)

direction
of pile

Shorts (cut 2)

fold line

fold line

fold line

fold line

Martha
(see pages 44–49)

Tummy patch
(cut 1 as appliqué)

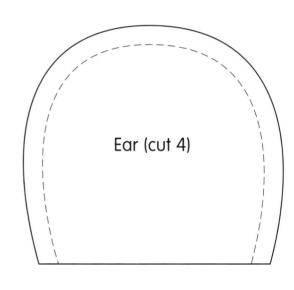

Arm (cut 2)

direction
of pile

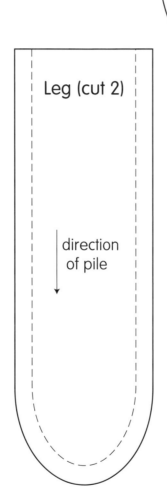

Leg (cut 2)

direction
of pile

Ear (cut 4)

Inner eye
(cut 2)

Outer eye
(cut 2)

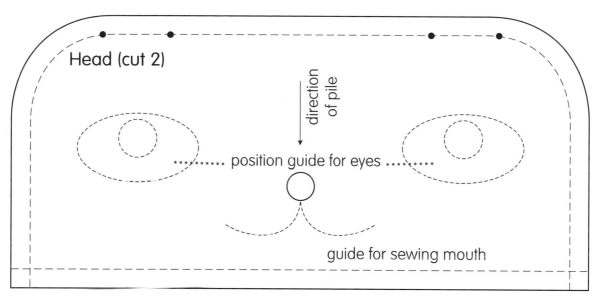

Head (cut 2)

direction
of pile

··········· position guide for eyes ··········

guide for sewing mouth

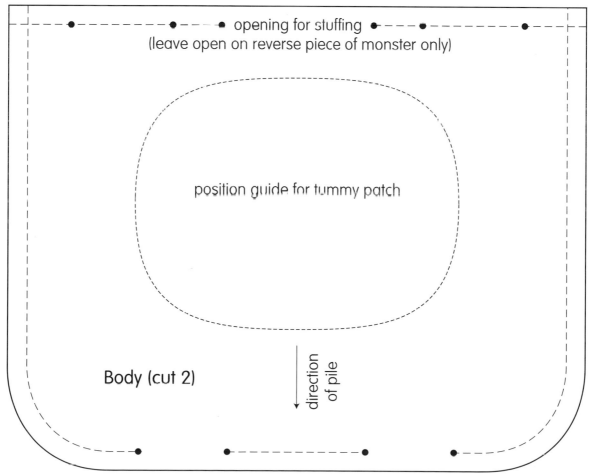

opening for stuffing
(leave open on reverse piece of monster only)

position guide for tummy patch

Body (cut 2)

direction
of pile

Dinah
(see pages 50–53)

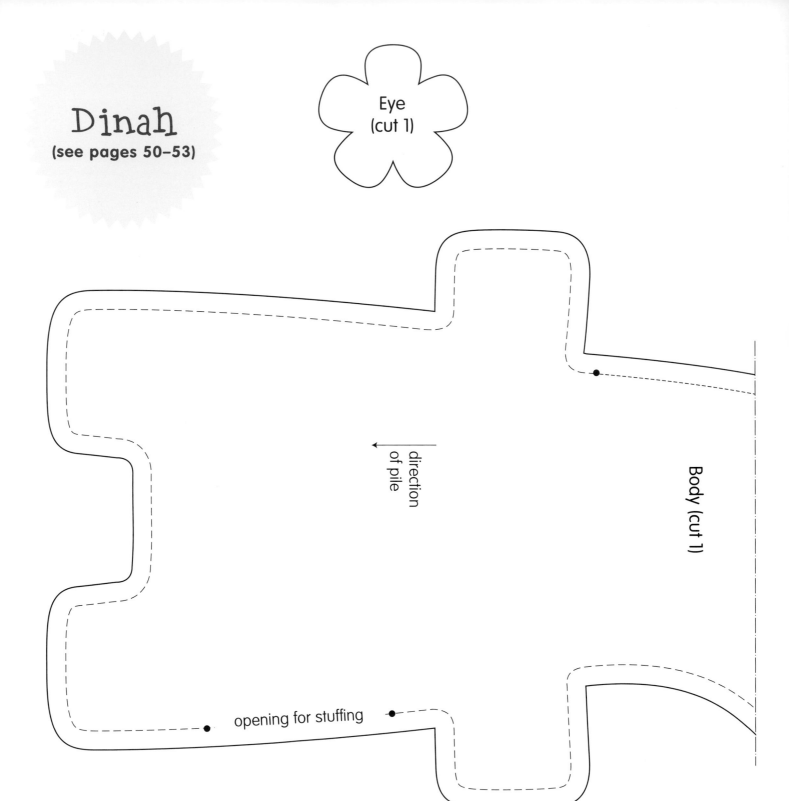

Eye
(cut 1)

direction
of pile

Body (cut 1)

opening for stuffing

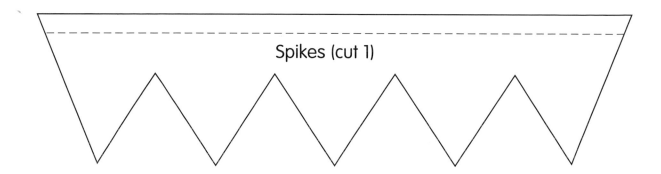

Spikes (cut 1)

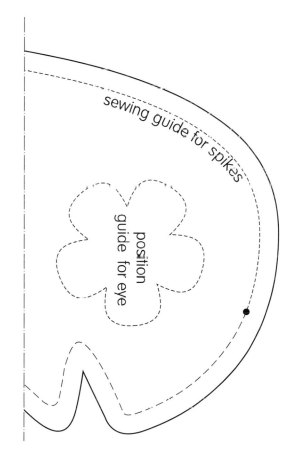

sewing guide for spikes

position guide for eye

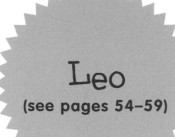

Leo
(see pages 54–59)

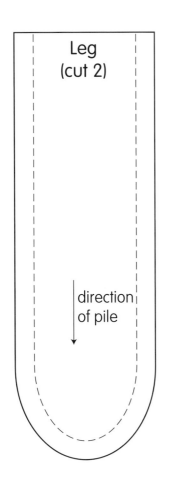

Leg
(cut 2)

direction
of pile

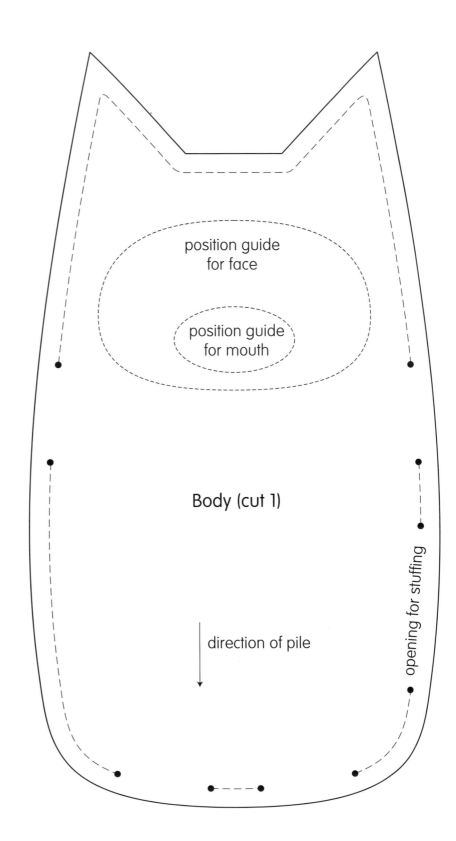

position guide
for face

position guide
for mouth

Body (cut 1)

direction of pile

opening for stuffing

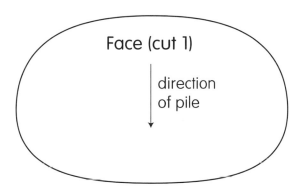

Face (cut 1)

direction
of pile

Mouth (cut 1)

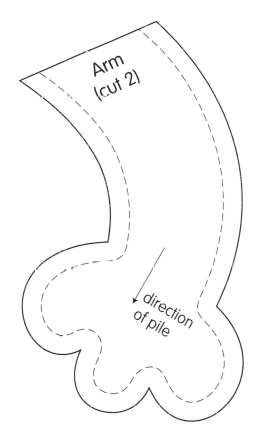

Arm
(cut 2)

direction
of pile

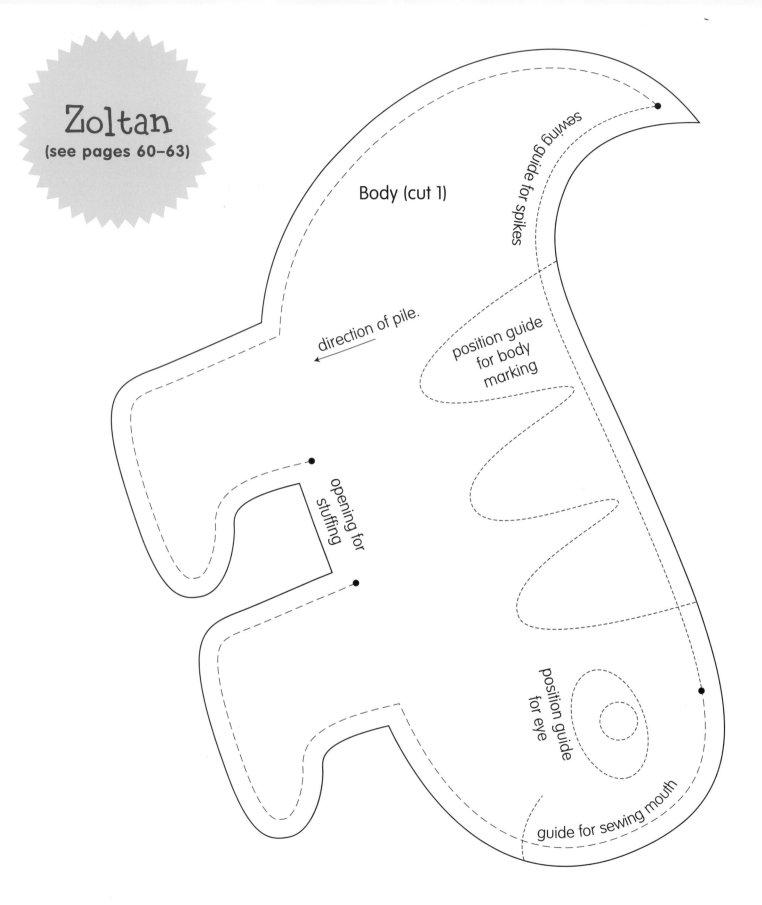

Zoltan
(see pages 60–63)

Body (cut 1)

sewing guide for spikes

direction of pile.

position guide for body marking

opening for stuffing

position guide for eye

guide for sewing mouth

Outer eye
(cut 1)

Inner eye (cut 1)

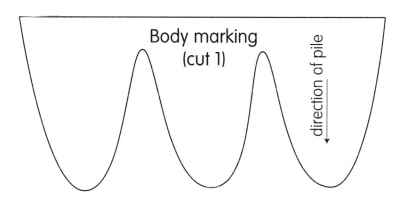

Body marking
(cut 1)

direction of pile

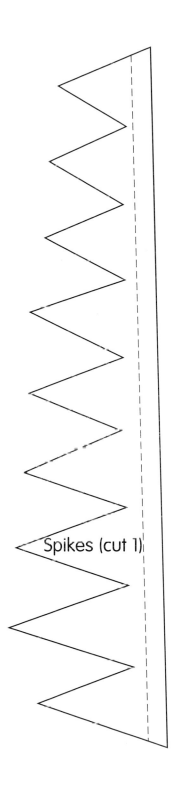

Spikes (cut 1)

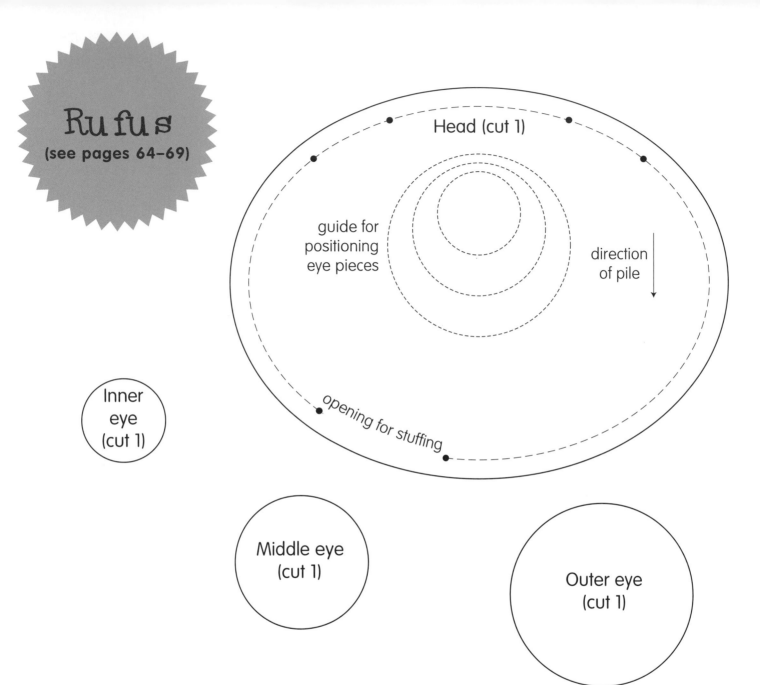

Rufus
(see pages 64–69)

Head (cut 1)

guide for
positioning
eye pieces

direction
of pile

opening for stuffing

Inner
eye
(cut 1)

Middle eye
(cut 1)

Outer eye
(cut 1)

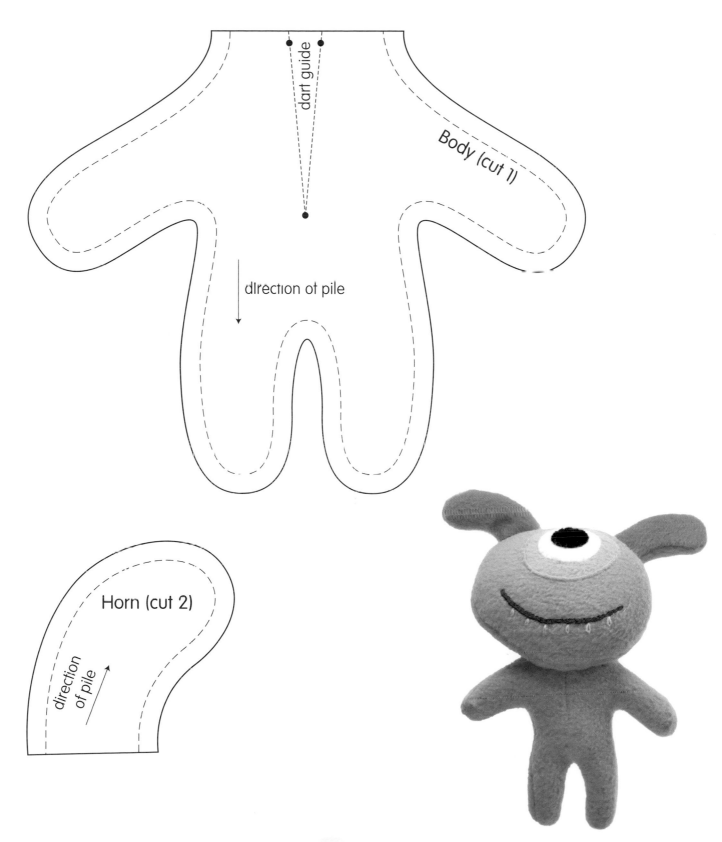

dart guide

Body (cut 1)

direction of pile

Horn (cut 2)

direction
of pile

Albert

(see pages 70–75)

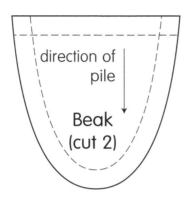

direction of
pile

**Beak
(cut 2)**

direction
of pile

Wing (cut 2)

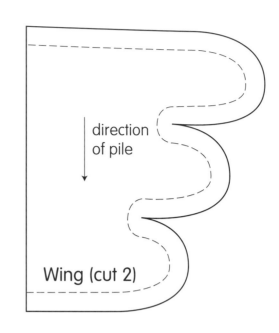

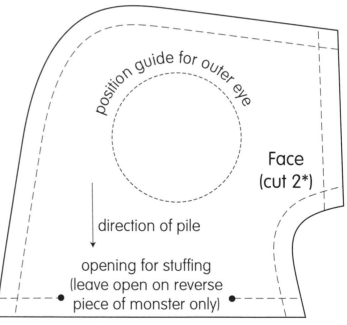

position guide for outer eye

direction of pile

opening for stuffing
(leave open on reverse
piece of monster only)

**Face
(cut 2*)**

* cut 1 piece using the template face up and
the other using the template face down

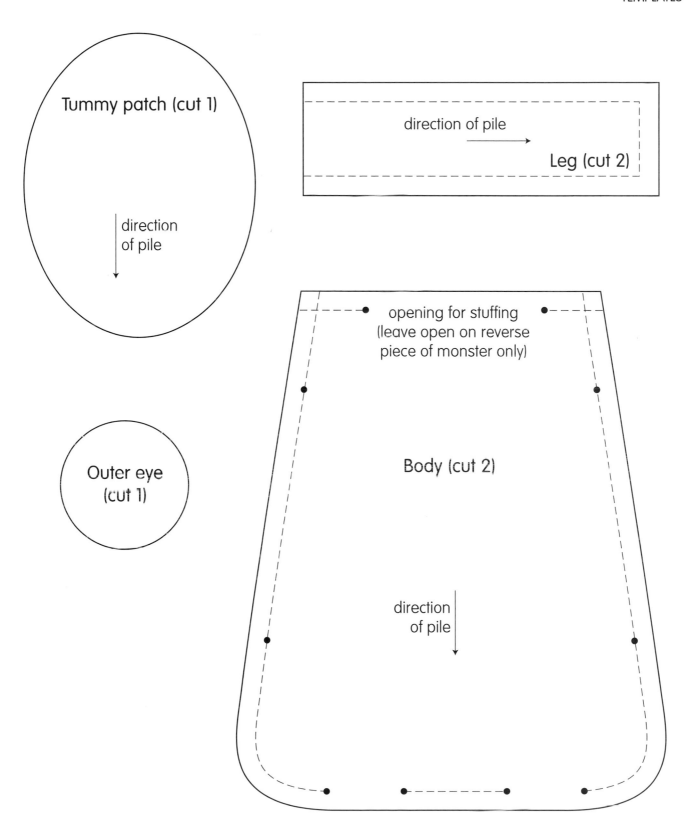

Tummy patch (cut 1)

direction
of pile

direction of pile

Leg (cut 2)

Outer eye
(cut 1)

opening for stuffing
(leave open on reverse
piece of monster only)

Body (cut 2)

direction
of pile

Dotty
(see pages 76–79)

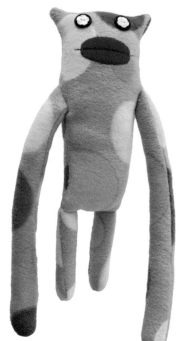

Lips (cut 1)

direction of
pile

opening for
stuffing

position guide for lips

Body (cut 1)

direction of pile

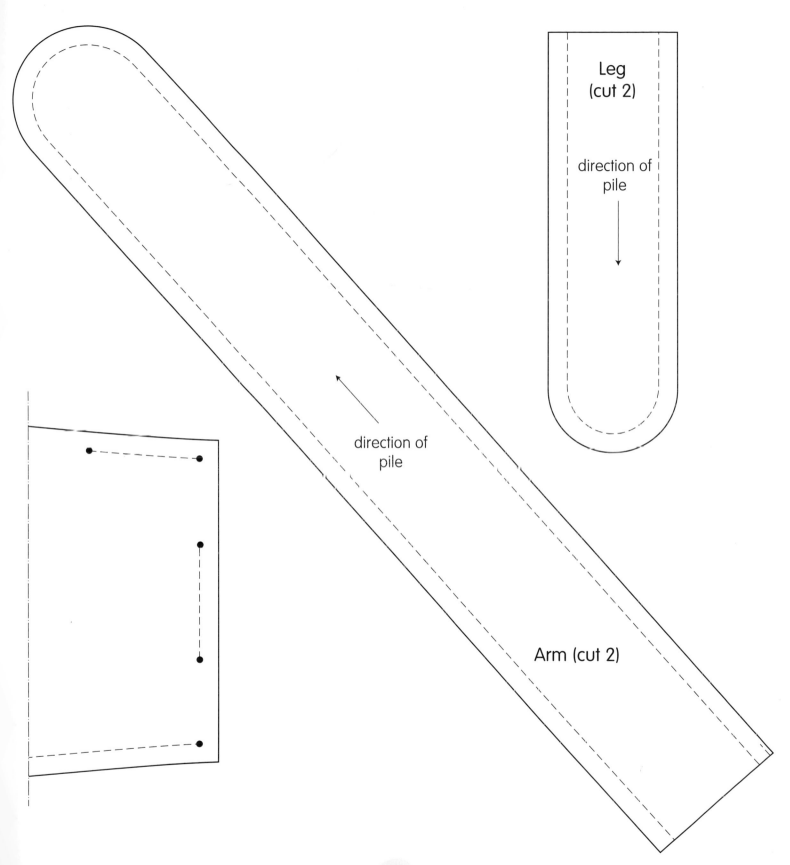

Leg
(cut 2)

direction of
pile

direction of
pile

Arm (cut 2)

Beatrice

(see pages 80–85)

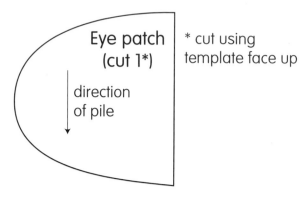

Eye patch
(cut 1*)

* cut using template face up

direction
of pile

Mouth (cut 1)

direction of pile

Leg (cut 2)

direction of pile

Arm (cut 2)

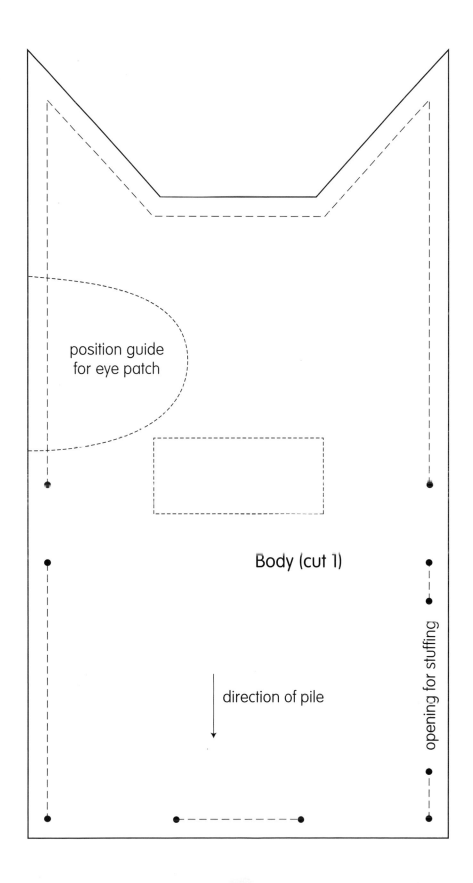

position guide
for eye patch

Body (cut 1)

direction of pile

opening for stuffing

Mini Monsters

(see pages 86–91)

Prudence face (cut 1)

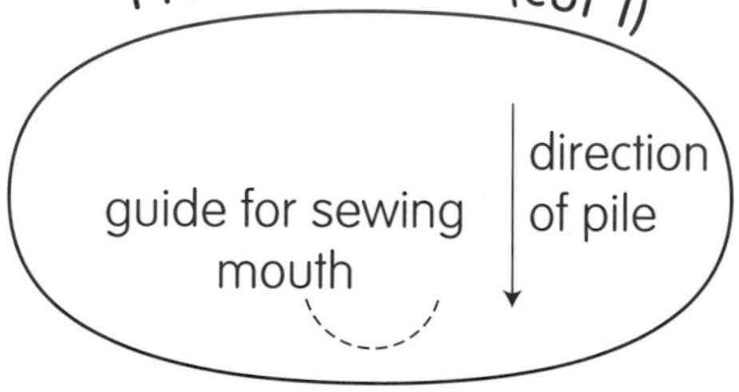

direction
of pile
guide for sewing
mouth

Eye (cut 2)

position guide for eyes
guide for
sewing mouth
position guide for face panel
Prudence body (cut 1)
direction of pile
opening for
stuffing

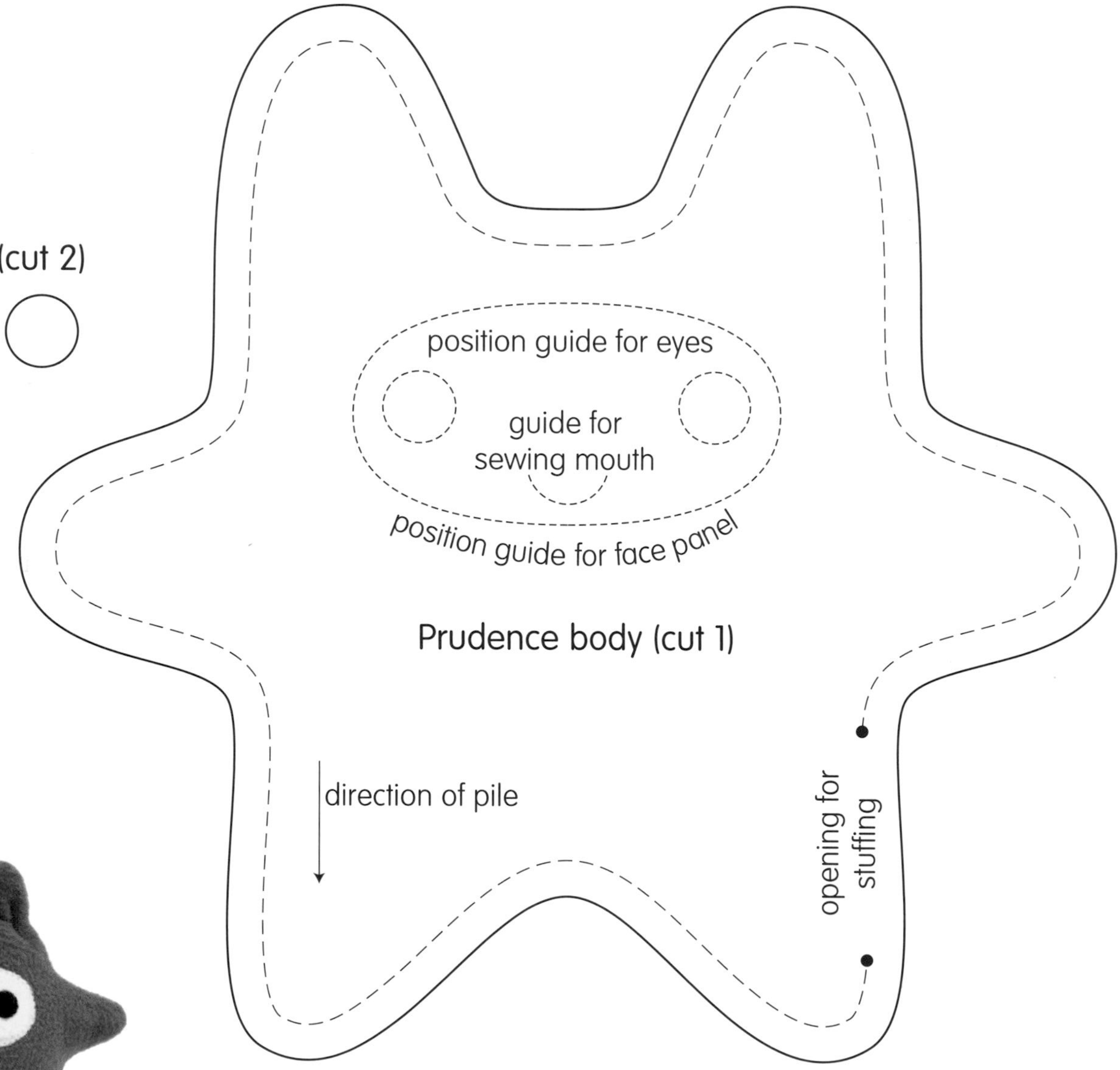

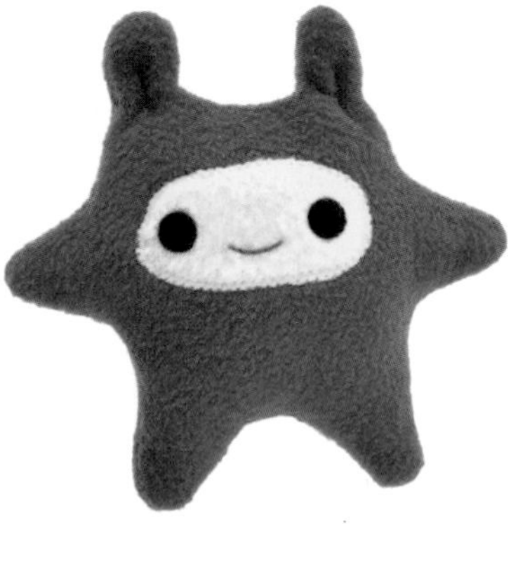

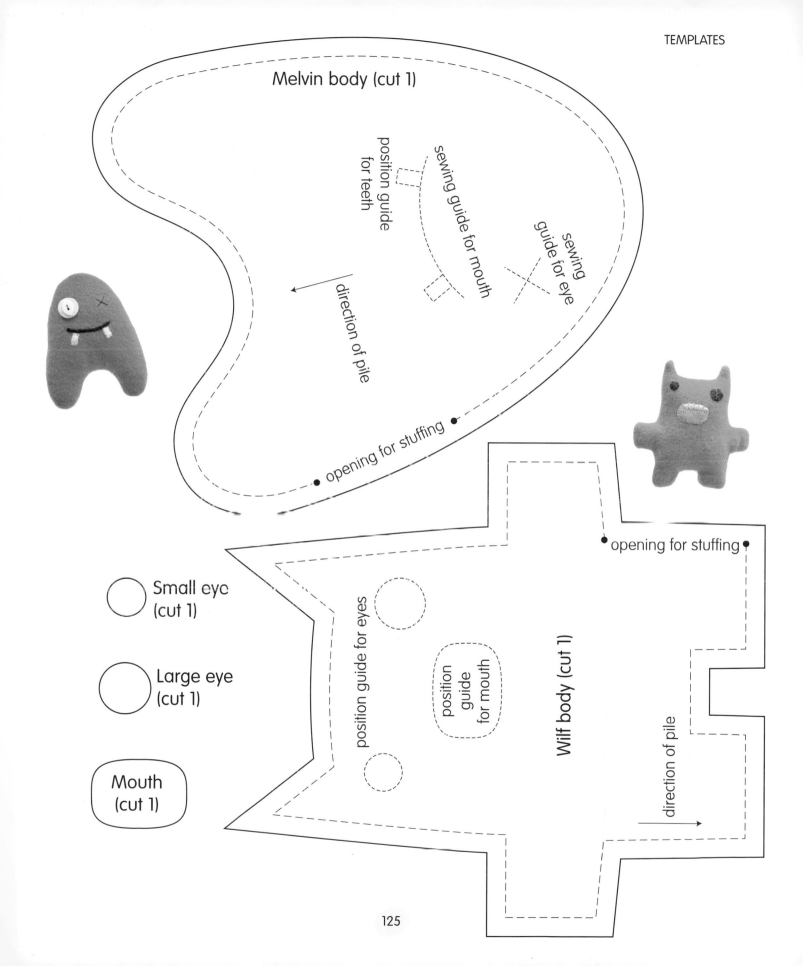

Melvin body (cut 1)

position guide for teeth

sewing guide for mouth

sewing guide for eye

direction of pile

opening for stuffing

opening for stuffing

Small eye (cut 1)

Large eye (cut 1)

Mouth (cut 1)

position guide for eyes

position guide for mouth

Wilf body (cut 1)

direction of pile

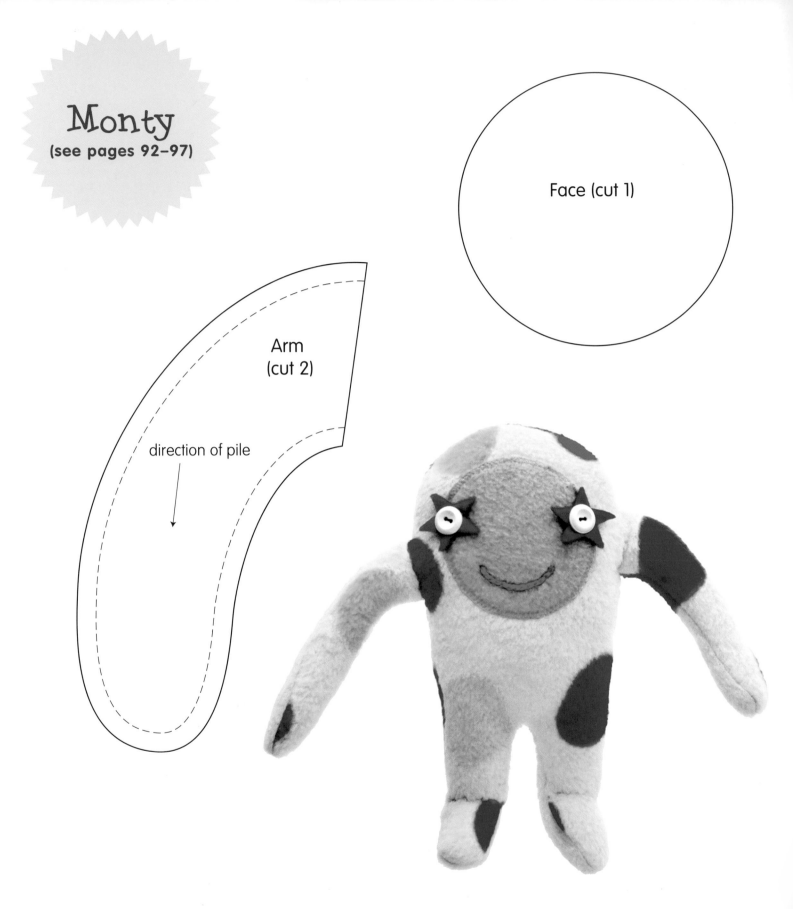

Monty
(see pages 92–97)

Face (cut 1)

Arm
(cut 2)

direction of pile

126

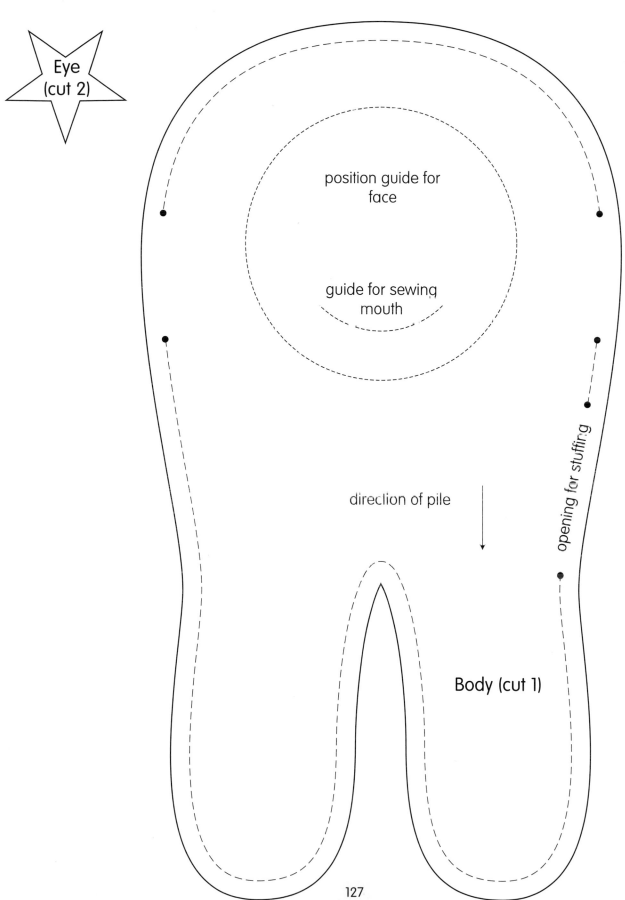

Eye
(cut 2)

position guide for
face

guide for sewing
mouth

direction of pile

opening for stuffing

Body (cut 1)

127

SUPPLIERS

This is a list of some of the UK stores, mail order companies and online companies that I have used when buying fleece, other fabrics and haberdashery items.

Abakhan Fabrics Hobby & Home,& Abakhan-Online Shop
Coast Road
Llanerch-Y-Mor
Mostyn, Flintshire
CH8 9DX
Tel: 01745 562101 (shop)
www.abakhan.co.uk
Fleece, other fabrics and haberdashery. Seven branches in the North West and online ordering service. See website for details of shop locations.

Calico Laine
Calico Laine
16 Liscard Crescent
Liscard, Wirral
CH44 1AE
Tel: 0151 638 6498 (shop)
Tel: 0151 336 3939 (enquiries)
www.calicolaine.co.uk
Fleece, other fabrics and haberdashery. Shop in person, by mail order or online.

Fabric Land
Fabric Land Ltd
Fabric Towers
Kingfisher Park
Headland, Salisbury Road
Ringwood, Hampshire
BH24 3NX
Tel: 01425 461444
www.fabricland.co.uk
Fleece, other fabrics and haberdashery. Order by phone or online. Eleven shops throughout the South.

Fabric UK
132 Satley Road
Birmingham
B7 4TH
Tel: 0121 359 7784
Freephone: 0800 170 1107
Email: kbt@fabricuk.com
www.fabricuk.com
Fleece, other fabrics and haberdashery. Shop in person or order online.

Fred Aldous
37 Lever Street
Manchester
M1 1LW
Tel: 0161 236 4224
www.fredaldous.co.uk
Craft products including felt and polyester toy stuffing. Shop in person, by phone or online.

Hobbycraft
HobbyCraft Group Limited
7 Enterprise Way
Aviation Park
Bournemouth International Airport
Christchurch, Dorset
BH23 6HG
Tel: 01202 596100
Freephone: 0800 027 2387
www.hobbycraft.co.uk
Haberdashery and craft items. Over 40 stores in the UK. Shop in person or order online. See website to submit email enquiry. Phone or see website to find your nearest store.

John Lewis
Tel: 08456 049 049
www.johnlewis.com
Department stores throughout the UK with haberdashery section. A small number of stores also sell fabrics. Phone or see website to find a store near you.

INDEX